FOUCAULT AGAINST NEOLIBERALISM?

FOUCAULT AGAINST NEOLIBERALISM?

Geoffroy de Lagasnerie

Translated by Matthew MacLellan

ROWMAN & LITTLEFIELD
Lanham • Boulder • New York • London

Epigraph from Michel Foucault, *The Archaeology of Knowledge*, trans. A. M. Sheridan Smith (New York: Pantheon).

Published by Rowman & Littlefield
An imprint of The Rowman & Littlefield Publishing Group, Inc.
4501 Forbes Boulevard, Suite 200, Lanham, Maryland 20706
https://rowman.com

6 Tinworth Street, London SE11 5AL, United Kingdom

British Library Cataloguing in Publication Information Available

Library of Congress Cataloging-in-Publication Data

Names: Lagasnerie, Geoffroy de, author. | MacLellan, Matthew, translator.
Title: Foucault against neoliberalism? / Geoffroy de Lagasnerie ; translated by Matthew MacLellan.
Other titles: Dernière leçon de Michel Foucault. English
Description: Lanham : Rowman & Littlefield, 2020. | "Original French publication of [La dernière leçon de Michel Foucault]. " | Includes bibliographical references and index. | Summary: "Michel Foucault was not seduced by neoliberalism: he wanted to discover its singularity in order to understand its appeal"-- Provided by publisher.
Identifiers: LCCN 2020003695 (print) | LCCN 2020003696 (ebook) | ISBN 9781786615275 (cloth) | ISBN 9781786616494 (paperback) | ISBN 9781786615282 (epub)
Subjects: LCSH: Foucault, Michel, 1926-1984--Political and social views. | Neoliberalism. | Political science--Philosophy.
Classification: LCC JC261.F68 L3413 2020 (print) | LCC JC261.F68 (ebook) | DDC 320.51/3--dc23
LC record available at https://lccn.loc.gov/2020003695
LC ebook record available at https://lccn.loc.gov/2020003696

"Rather than founding a theory . . .
my present concern is to establish a possibility."

—Michel Foucault

CONTENTS

TRANSLATOR'S PREFACE

Geoffroy de Lagasnerie's *La dernière leçon de Michel Foucault* was one of the first books dedicated to Michel Foucault's controversial lectures on neoliberalism at the Collège de France in 1978 and 1979. Foucault's ambiguous relationship to neoliberalism, as well as his ostensible turn away from the political left in the later years of his life, has since become an increasingly prominent topic of discussion and debate among Foucault scholars in Europe and North America, and several scholarly editions have since appeared that critically examine both topics directly. Because the original French publication of *La dernière leçon de Michel Foucault* predates much of the recent discussion on the problem of Foucault's neoliberalism, it is worth taking some time to situate the book's English translation within this larger and growing conversation.

It is no secret that Michel Foucault was purposefully ambiguous about his political allegiances, and one would be hard pressed to find another thinker as resistant to labels—political or otherwise—as he. In an interview at Berkeley in 1983, Foucault responded to questions about his political leanings by emphasizing how he had been considered, at various times in his career, "an enemy by the Marxists, an enemy by the right wing, and an enemy of people in the center," largely because the projects he pursued and the questions he asked were not "determined by a pre-established political outlook and [did] not tend toward the realization of some definite political project."[1] As his close friend and colleague George Dumézil famously put it, Foucault "wore masks, and he was always changing them." Foucault grew up in a wealthy family in the provincial French city of Poitiers, and yet he, along with most of his peers at the École Normale Supérior, joined the French Communist Party (PCF) in 1950 under the influence of their teacher, Louis Althusser. But Foucault was never a committed party member or activist, and he officially left the PCF in 1953 due to the excesses of Stalinism and, likely, the PCF's rigid condemnation of homosexuality. While teaching at the University of Clermont-Ferrand years later, Foucault explicitly described himself as an "anarchist of the left," and yet during his time at the University of Tunis, students frequently took Foucault to be a right-wing Gaullist because of his consistent denunciations of official Marxism and his continual reference to Nietzsche in all of his lectures.[2]

Yet the image of Michel Foucault that is most deeply engrained in the popular and academic imagination is the "ultra-left" militant intellectual he became in the late 1960s and early 1970s during his brief tenure as the head of the philosophy department at the Centre Expérimental de Vincennes (now the University of Paris VIII) and his first years occupying the chair in The History of Systems of Thought at the Collège de France. While at Vincennes, from 1968 to 1970, Foucault frequently participated in student strikes and demonstrations, and he was often present during violent clashes with police. And from 1971 to 1976, after he was elected to the summit of the French academy, Foucault's public fame rose further still through his public activism in, and indeed leadership of, the *Group d'Information sur les Prisons*, an activist organization that exposed the poor conditions of French prisons, advocated for prison reform, and tried to give voice to the incarcerated in French society without assuming to speak for them. During these years, Foucault circulated

---

1. "Politics and Ethics: An Interview." In *The Foucault Reader*, edited by Paul Rabinow (New York: Vintage Books, 2010), 375.
2. See Didier Eribon, *Michel Foucault*, translated by Betsy Wing (Cambridge: Harvard University Press, 1991).

pamphlets and petitions, was frequently featured on French television and in the press, marched in protests, and manned barricades alongside some of France's most prominent public intellectuals, such as Jean-Paul Sartre, Jean Genet, and Gilles Deleuze. It was during this intense period of activism that Foucault arguably supplanted Sartre as France's most recognized and important public intellectual, and even after the *Group d'Information sur les Prisons* disbanded in 1976, the image of Foucault as France's premier leftist thinker, whose prose "furnishes weapons for contemporary struggles," was rarely questioned, particularly in North America after the importation of "French theory" in the 1980s and 1990s.[3]

Yet it is precisely this image of Foucault as a committed leftist theorist and activist that recent scholarship has begun to question, and largely on the basis of Foucault's lectures on neoliberalism in 1978 and 1979 (somewhat confusingly titled *The Birth of Biopolitics*).[4] What we might call the "seduction thesis"—or the claim that Foucault was "seduced by some of [neoliberalism's] key ideas"[5]—contends that Foucault's engagement with neoliberalism was not only indicative of a more general rightward turn in his own political disposition, but his embrace of neoliberalism played an important role in the larger rejection of left radicalism in French intellectual and political life in the late 1970s, all of which scholarship on Foucault has, over the years, tended to either downplay or avoid altogether. For better or worse, the main thrust of this new scholarship asserts the necessity of seriously confronting Foucault's embrace of neoliberalism and his seeming support of a whole range of rightwing, free-market reforms in the late 1970s and early 1980s.

---

3. See François Cusset, *French Theory: How Foucault, Derrida, Deleuze, & Co. Transformed the Intellectual Life of the United States*, translated by Jeff Fort (Minneapolis: University of Minnesota Press, 2008).

4. As Foucault admits in the *Annuaire de Collège de France*, the lectures in 1978 and 1979 "[were] to have been about biopolitics . . . [but] ended up being devoted entirely to what should have been [biopolitic's] introduction." Michel Foucault, *The Birth of Biopolitics: Lectures at the Collège de France, 1978-1979*, translated by Graham Burchell (New York: Palgrave Macmillan, 2008), 317.

5. Daniel Zamora, "Introduction: Foucault, the Left, and the 1980s." In *Foucault and Neoliberalism*, edited by Daniel Zamora and Michael C. Behrent (London: Polity, 2016), 2–3.

The claim that Foucault's lectures on neoliberalism are conspicuously lacking the usual criticism or hostility one typically encounters in leftist analyses of neoliberalism is not in itself new. As Colin Gordon observed in 1991, "Foucault's account of the liberal and neo-liberal thinkers indeed often evinces a sense of (albeit value-neutral) intellectual attraction and esteem":

> He suggests that recent neo-liberalism, understood (as he proposes) as a novel set of notions about the art of government, is a considerably more original and challenging phenomenon than the left's critical culture has had the courage to acknowledge, and that its political challenge is one the left is singularly ill equipped to respond to, the more so since, as Foucault contends, socialism itself does not possess and has never possessed its own distinctive art of governing.[6]

Although Gordon's brief and hedged comments on Foucault's neoliberalism (i.e., his parenthetical use of the "value-neutral" adjective) are little more than an aside within his larger description of Foucault's studies on governmentality, they nonetheless provide a crucial contextualizing element for understanding Foucault's interest in neoliberalism: namely, socialism's inability to generate or invent a governmental rationality of its own. Virtually all the recent scholarship on Foucault's relationship to neoliberalism echoes Gordon's prior claim that Foucault's engagement with neoliberalism in his 1978 and 1979 lectures was determined, to some degree, by Foucault's assessment of the political sterility of socialism in France during this period, particularly the policies that made up the "common program" proposed by the coalition of the Socialist Party, the PCF, and the Radical Movement of the Left in 1972, many of which were implemented (however briefly) after the electoral victory of the Socialists under the leadership of François Mitterrand in 1981. The crux of the recent debate, then, turns on what Foucault's en-

---

6. Colin Gordon, "Governmental Rationality: An Introduction." In *The Foucault Effect*, edited by Graham Burchell, Colin Gordon, and Peter Miller (Chicago: University of Chicago Press, 1991), 6.

gagement with neoliberalism was meant to accomplish: was his
analysis of neoliberalism an attempt to reinvigorate leftist politics in
France, or did Foucault more straightforwardly abandon the left in
favor of a more rightward and market-friendly political posture?
That Foucault might have been wary of or even hostile toward
traditional socialist ideas, particularly the prominent role of the state
in revolutionary socialism, is, in the first instance, entirely congru-
ent with the analytic of modern power Foucault developed in the
1970s. Whereas it would be somewhat reductive to refer to Foucault
as an anti-statist thinker—Foucault in fact warns his audience during his lectures on neoliberalism precisely against succumbing to
the simplistic and paranoid "state-phobia" that afflicted many of the
twentieth century's more influential neoliberals[7]—Foucault's novel
and penetrating genealogy of modern power was at base an attempt
to theorize the proliferation and encroachment of what might loose-
ly be referred to as state administrative institutions—hospitals, clin-
ics, prisons, schools, etc.—into the pores of social life, and the
concomitant rationalities, processes, and practices of discipline and
normalization they deployed in order to create the *sui generis* subjects of Western modernity. Against the comparatively cruder and
concomitantly more abstract Marxist categories that tend to conceptualize power in terms of "a general system of domination exerted
by one group over another,"[8] Foucault's genealogy of modern power focused much more narrowly on the concrete but diffuse techniques, rationalities, and practices that generated modern subjects
not merely through a process of "objectification" (negative power
that functions through repression and interdiction) but "subjectifica-
tion" (positive or productive power in which the subject itself plays
an active role).[9] By carefully studying a range of seemingly marginal or contingent techniques and practices across entire networks of

7.   Michel Foucault, *The Birth of Biopolitics: Lectures at the Collège de France,
1978-79*, translated by Graham Burchell (New York: Palgrave Macmillan, 2008), 76.
8.   Michel Foucault, *The History of Sexuality: An Introduction*, translated by Robert
Hurley (New York: Vintage Books, 1978), 92.
9.   This terminology is borrowed from Paul Rabinow's introduction to *The Foucault
Reader* (New York: Vintage Books, 1984).

modern institutions or *dispositifs*, Foucault documented the gradual decline of an older, sovereign technology of power that "drives out, excludes, banishes, marginalizes, and represses," and mapped the ascendency of a new, modern form of disciplinary power that is "fundamentally positive" and "fashions, observes, knows, and multiplies itself on the basis of its own effects."[10] Although it may be technically inaccurate, therefore, to describe Foucault as an anti-statist thinker insofar as the state, *qua* politico-juridical entity, was never really the principal focus of his analysis in the first place, his genealogy of modern power nonetheless disclosed "the rise of the social"[11] as a new and expanding governmental domain of supervision, administration, regulation, and normalization.

The constitutive "problematic" to which Foucault's account of modern power responded was thus profoundly different from the problematic that shapes the political project of the contemporary left. After forty years of sustained neoliberal assault from across the political spectrum, leftist politics today (especially in the United States) is largely conditioned by the overall *absence* or *weakness* of state institutions, particularly state institutions charged with social welfare functions (as opposed to those charged with police and military roles; in these matters, the American state has been anything but weak). Rather than confronting a political situation conditioned by the relative weakness of state institutions, Foucault's account of disciplinary power emerged instead at a time when "European welfare states still appeared to be the beacon and future of the civilized West, and the question for most of those leaning left in the mid-1970s was not how to defend them."[12] One of the most pressing concerns for those engaged in social and political critique in the 1970s, then, was not the fragility of the welfare state (though perhaps it ought to have been) but rather the unintended and underthe-

---

10. Michel Foucault, *Abnormal: Lectures at the Collège de France, 1974-1975*, translated by Graham Burchell (New York: Picador, 2003), 48.
11. See Gilles Deleuze, "Foreword: The Rise of the Social." In Jacques Donzelot, *The Policing of Families*, translated by Robert Hurley (New York: Pantheon Books, 1979).
12. Wendy Brown, *Undoing the Demos: Neoliberalism's Stealth Revolution* (New York: Zone Books, 2015), 51.

orized consequences of the precipitous rise in "governmentality" that accompanied the vast expansion of welfare state institutions in the postwar period. Following the publication of *Discipline and Punish* in 1975, then, Foucault's lectures at the Collège de France during the mid- to late 1970s pivoted toward a more capacious endeavor to develop a "theory and analysis of everything 'that tends to affirm and increase the power of the state, to make good use of its forces, to procure the happiness of its subjects' and chiefly 'the maintenance of order and discipline.'"[13] By shifting his analysis of power toward a concern for "governmentality," Foucault was able to argue, among much else, that state socialism was far less revolutionary than was often claimed, precisely because it lacked its own governmental rationality, its own "art of government." As Foucault argued, "I would say that what socialism lacks is not so much a theory of the state as a governmental reason, [or] the definition of what a governmental rationality would be in socialism":

> In actual fact, and history has shown this, socialism can only be implemented [by connecting] up to diverse types of governmentality. It has been connected up to liberal governmentality [and] we have seen it function, and still see it function, within governmentalities that would no doubt fall more under what last year we called the police state [in which] socialism functions as the internal logic of an administrative apparatus. Maybe there are still other governmentalities that socialism is connected up to; it remains to be seen. But in any case, I do not think that for the moment there is an autonomous governmentality of socialism.[14]

While the concept of "governmentality" proffered Foucault a conceptually powerful framework through which to critique traditional socialist practices and policies, he was hardly alone in assuming this critical stance toward socialism during this period. Critique of the traditional French left, especially the PCF, was a defining feature of

---

13. Michel Foucault, "Course Summary." In *Security, Territory, Population: Lectures at the Collège de France, 1977-78*, translated by Graham Burchell (New York: Picador, 2007), 366.

14. Foucault, *The Birth of Biopolitics*, 91–93.

May 1968, and the generation that lived through this tumultuous period soon after looked upon the privileged organs of the traditional left—the party and the union in particular—as bureaucratic and even disciplinary institutions that were just as suspect as the institutions of the political right (the military, police, church, etc.). This shift in France's political culture thus saw the emergence of a "second left" in the mid-1970s, led by figures such as Michel Rocard, Pierre Rosanvallon, and Patrick Viveret, which was dedicated to undermining the centrality of the state in the French political imagination, and which called for a new culture of political creativity and inventiveness that pushed left politics beyond the simple nationalizing of industry and the hierarchical centrality of the party in the state. And at the same time that this second left was challenging traditional socialist ideas in order to create a new kind of leftist politics, a much more polemical strain of political commentary was simultaneously condemning any socialist policies whatsoever as nothing less than a step toward the gulag. Spurred on by rising international concern over Soviet dissidents as well as the publication of Alexander Solzhenitsyn's *The Gulag Archipelago* in 1974, these "new philosophers"—most notably the former Maoist André Glucksmann and Bernard Henri-Lévy—published a series of best-selling books that linked any and all forms of Marxism and socialism with the worst excesses of Stalinism.[15] While Foucault influentially endorsed the general project of the second left in a variety of interviews and talks, he more consequentially wrote a very favorable review of André Glucksmann's *Les maitres penseurs* (*The Master Thinkers*, 1977)—arguably the most polemical attack on Marxism by the new philosophers—in *Le Nouvel Observateur*, a widely read French weekly. In addition to endowing the new philosophers with a great deal of intellectual prestige, Foucault's review would also become the catalyst for the permanent split between Foucault and Gilles Deleuze (who contrastingly viewed the new philosophers as little more than vapid television celebrities).

---

15.   See Michael Scott Christofferson, *French Intellectuals Against the Left: the Anti-totalitarian Movement of the 1970s* (New York: Berghahn Books, 2004).

Foucault's genealogical account of disciplinary power, his sub-
sequent pivot toward the study of governmentality, and the more
general turn away from Marxism and socialism in French intellectual culture, thus constitute the background context against which
Foucault, in the late 1970s, became increasingly interested in a very
new and different political rationality that had been inconspicuously
nurtured on the margins of Western intellectualism throughout the
twentieth century.[16] Whatever Foucault's intentions in these lectures, virtually all the scholarship on the subject agrees there is
much that is *prima facie* singular about Foucault's engagement with
neoliberalism. In none of his prior lectures or published books did
Foucault directly address contemporary politics to the extent he
does in these lectures. Nor, interestingly, does Foucault's investigation of neoliberalism hew to the genealogical method he so success-
fully developed and applied in *Discipline and Punish*. Instead of
examining the marginal but concrete techniques that collectively
constitute—or not, as the case may be—a coherent rationality or
logic of power, Foucault gives us something much more akin to a
traditional history of ideas (perhaps because neoliberalism was
more ideational than technical prior to the 1980s). And lastly—and
on this point the scholarship on Foucault's neoliberalism is in complete agreement—Foucault was remarkably prescient in perceiving
neoliberalism, prior to the 1980s, as a new and highly original form
of governmental rationality that deserves our serious intellectual
attention and scrutiny. Exactly why, or to what ends, Foucault
thought we ought to scrutinize neoliberalism is, however, where the
agreement ends and the scholarly debate begins. Although we may
have always intuitively sensed Foucault's "politics are emancipatory," Michael Behrent argues we have tended to be somewhat "tone-
deaf" about the "deep affinity between Foucault's thought and neo-

---

16.   See Philip Mirowski and Dieter Plehwe, eds., *The Road From Mont Pèlerin: The
Making of the Neoliberal Thought Collective* (Cambridge: Harvard University Press,
2009).

liberalism," particularly their "shared suspicion of the state."[17] For Pierre Dardot and Christian Laval, on the other hand, Foucault's lectures on neoliberalism provide us with more precise conceptual tools for challenging the neoliberal revolution itself. Whereas the Marxist interpretation of neoliberalism had "not always understood that the crisis of the 1960s and 1970s is not reducible to an 'economic crisis' in the classical sense," Foucault, argue Dardot and Laval, was much more successful in theorizing the nuanced manner in which the political, economic, and cultural dimensions of life were "in the process of discovering a potential consistency, theoretical and practical, with neo-liberalism."[18] Whereas Wendy Brown considers claims about Foucault's deep attraction to neoliberalism as rather overstated, she also rejects the contrary interpretation that "Foucault is offering a neo-Marxist critique of neoliberal rationality in these lectures." For Brown, Foucault was primarily interested in "neoliberalism's transformation of the social, the state, and the subject, and also how neoliberalism brings liberalism more squarely into places, such as France, where liberal principles had heretofore nested somewhat uneasily with other governing rationalities, such as republicanism and socialism."[19] And according to Daniel Zamora, Foucault not only failed to anticipate the future consequences of the neoliberal transformation, but he seemed to have "almost encouraged [it] in the name of greater autonomy and the subject's rebellion against major institutional structures."[20]

Such are but a few of the diverse and divergent interpretations that currently circulate within the growing scholarly discussion of Foucault's neoliberalism. And while this conversation has undoubtedly become increasingly engaging and productive in recent years,

---

17. Michael C. Behrent, "Liberalism Without Humanism: Michel Foucault and the Free Market Creed, 1976-1979," *Modern Intellectual History*, vol. 3, no. 6, (2009), 541, 545. Reprinted in *Foucault and Neoliberalism*, edited by Zamora and Behrent (London: Polity, 2016).
18. Pierre Dardot and Christian Laval, *The New Way of the World: On Neo-Liberal Society*, translated by Gregory Elliott (London: Verso, 2013), 11.
19. Wendy Brown, *Undoing the Demos*, 55–56.
20. Daniel Zamora, "Foucault and the Excluded." In *Foucault and Neoliberalism*, edited by Daniel Zamora and Michael C. Behrent (London: Polity, 2016), 64.

it has proceeded, at least in the English-speaking scholarship, without direct access to one of the debate's earliest and most formative voices. Geoffroy de Lagasnerie's compelling reading of Foucault's neoliberalism is frequently mentioned in introductions on the subject, and his original French text, *La dernière leçon de Michel Foucault*, is regularly cited by some of the most prominent voices in this debate. But for most English readers, the text itself has remained inaccessible. I have therefore endeavored to offer English readers as faithful a translation of Lagasnerie's influential book as possible, in the interest of rendering his previously implicit contribution explicit, and thereby further enriching our ongoing conversations about Foucault's most controversial lectures. The English title of Lagasnerie's text reflects this intent. As Lagasnerie convincingly argues in the pages that follow, our engagement with Foucault's lectures on neoliberalism should not be limited to a debate over Foucault's personal intentions or political aspirations—whether he was *for* or *against* neoliberalism. We must focus instead on what Foucault's search for the singularity of neoliberalism can teach us about our political preconceptions, and how his inquiry into neoliberalism can still help us reconstitute a critical leftist project under our own very different political realities.

Matthew MacLellan
Halifax, Nova Scotia,
2019

FOREWORD

The question of neoliberalism occupies an increasingly central position in contemporary thought. As we are constantly reminded in book after book, at conference after conference, denouncing the invasion of neoliberalism's logic is the essential challenge of our time. Neoliberalism is said to be transforming the way our world works. It is undoubtedly redefining the rules of the economy. But, more seriously, it is upending the traditional organization of society as a whole. The entire social order has been shaken by this overwhelming groundswell, and all the institutions upon which the social order rests—the state, schools, the family, the law, and so forth—are affected. An unprecedented way of conceiving the relations between the political, the legal, and the economic, as well as the relations between the individual and the collective, is beginning to crystalize, and it thus falls upon the humanities, as a matter of great urgency, to address this phenomenon in order to grasp its implications, assess its dangers, and offer instruments of resistance.

One would have hoped that so much attention paid to a single subject would have produced results that were particularly rich and inventive. Alas, we are rather witnessing the standardization and limitation of intellectual life. Superimposable analyses that mobilize the same perspectives, and the same frames of reference, circulate in virtually all sectors of the intellectual field. The neoliberal problematic, in other words, is accelerating the dissolution of theoretical and political divisions: instead of triggering a multiplicity of contradictory interpretations, neoliberalism elicits analogous sentiments among people whom we might have expected to take divergent, even opposite, positions. We are thus witnessing a narrowing of the thinkable and the speakable, and a reduction of potential alternatives. In short, we are experiencing a general crisis of the imagination.

The almost systematic gesture of innumerable contemporary texts devoted to denouncing neoliberalism is an argument that takes the form of a lament: today, everything that falls under the logic of "community" is being eroded on behalf of a logic of individuality and particularism. Neoliberalism is establishing the reign of egoism and a withdrawal into the self. It is prioritizing particular interests and the "I" to the detriment of the "we," the "social," and our common institutions. Morality, religion, politics, law, etc., have consequently lost their prescriptive and integrative force and relations of reciprocity, of the gift, and of assistance crumble and are, little by little, replaced by market relations. Individuals henceforth no longer submit themselves to any superior principle or essential, transcendent value in order to "make" or "re-make" society (such as shared norms or values, reciprocity, etc.). Neoliberalism has provoked a crisis of the "social bond" (disaffiliation), a crisis of mutual care and solidarity, and a multiplication of minority movements in which individuals demand special rights (what we often call democracy) and thereby express their refusal to submit to the symbolic order and to the law.

There is obviously much to be said about this discourse, about its lacunas and its limitations, and about the impulses animating its speakers. But what interests me in particular is the way in which this discourse discloses a transformation of leftist thought, specifically in terms of the prevailing temperament of contemporary critical theory. Indeed, this discourse testifies to the increasingly powerful influence of a dominant paradigm or, better, a mode of problematization: it buttresses a type of perception in which anomie, deregulation, disorder, and so forth, are all framed as negatives, and the "decomposition" of our societies, the "destruction" of the common world, and social "dilution" or "atomization" are all proffered as foils. This framework also inversely defines the restoration of "collective living," the desire to restore "meaning" to collective institutions, and the reconstruction of the "social bond" as positive necessities.

We need to be conscious, however, of the fact that such statements do not actually describe anything: they do not constitute serious analyses of the neoliberal phenomenon, nor of the ongoing transformations of society. They rather constitute a system of interpretation, or a matrix of intelligibility: they compel us to see the world in only one way—meaning other views are possible and other representations can be developed. The hegemony of this ideological structure also highlights the extent to which the left, and more notably the radical left, has been disoriented, distraught, and even bewildered by the advent of neoliberalism, and found itself powerless before the sudden emergence of this new paradigm. The political necessity to struggle against this form of governmentality has led to intellectual paralysis and even a kind of anti-intellectualism: the imperative to denounce neoliberalism comes first, and the rationale operating within these denunciations matters less. This makes it impossible for critical theory to even minimally reflect upon its own reasoning.

The outcome of this situation has been an inversion, if not a transmutation, of values: the contemporary left speaks the language of order, of the state, of regulation. This is why, it seems to me, we are confronted today with the necessity of reinventing the left. It is imperative for us to turn our backs on these older incantations and renounce the fantasies of regulation expressed through them. We must develop a new language of observation and create a new critical theory that does not function as a machine for denouncing materialism, consumerism, commodification, individualism, or, simply, freedom, to the point of lending undo praise to collective norms and institutional forms of transcendence.

Reviving what Pierre Bourdieu called "the left's libertarian tradition"[1] will not, of course, be realized through a polemical and strategic register alone. This book is not a manifesto. Yet the authoritarian impulses that have become manifest, and continue to be manifest, as a result of the struggle against neoliberalism did not emerge out of a vacuum. They are indications of a potentiality inscribed within the very conceptual architecture of social theory and political philosophy itself—and perhaps they have even been shaped and hailed by it. In any case, this *dispositif* must, necessarily, be an object that is examined, reworked, and reformulated. I've chosen to undertake this project through a rereading of the texts Michel Foucault devoted to neoliberalism (in particular his course at the Collège de France titled *The Birth of Biopolitics*) because, as I will demonstrate, Foucault reflected on an identical problem throughout these lectures: how to develop a radical theory, a critical philosophy, and an emancipatory practice in the era of neoliberalism.

---

1. Pierre Bourdieu, "Rediscovering the Left's Libertarian Tradition." In *Political Interventions: Social Science and Political Action*, translated by David Fernbach (London: Verso: 2008), 127–30.

INTRODUCTION

A TRANSGRESSION

Of all the courses given by Michel Foucault at the Collège de France, *The Birth of Biopolitics* is probably the most discussed, but it is almost certainly the most controversial, and for many reasons. This is because the analysis of neoliberalism Foucault offers, his reading of the principle theoreticians of this school, and his interpretation of the politics inspired by this doctrine, sewed much confusion: was Foucault, at the end of his life, in the process of becoming a liberal? Do his lectures indeed confirm that, sometime in the early 1980s, Foucault began to descend down a slippery slope? And should we not face the fact, as disturbing as it may be, that the author of *Discipline and Punish*, this central figure of the post–May 1968 radical left, was, on the eve of his death, about to take an unfortunate turn to the right—as would many of his disciples from this period?

Foucault's failure to utter even the slightest criticism of neoliberalism in these lectures—while he spares no criticism of Marxism and socialism—is often raised in support of this view. Foucault comments on neoliberal texts, he describes how the policies implemented by Helmut Schmidt in Germany and Valéry Giscard d'Estaing in France are inscribed within this intellectual tradition, but he never explicitly distances himself from these programs. In short, the tone of his book does not seem to be critical. The book unfolds as if Foucault was ensnared by his object, even fascinated by it. Rather than forging instruments of resistance against the neoliberal revolution descending upon the world, it was as if Foucault seemed content to merely describe its advent. His silence seems to imply tacit assent.

Yet this accusation against Foucault, it seems to me, must be explained otherwise. I argue it is the result of a more insidious, and perhaps more fundamental, phenomenon than is visible at first glance: by deciding to offer a course dedicated to the neoliberal tradition, Foucault in fact transgressed a deeply inscribed boundary within intellectual culture itself.

Over the course of the past sixty years, a kind of wall has been gradually built up separating legitimate or dominant theoretical space on the one side, and neoliberalism on the other. Accordingly, neoliberal theoreticians have been framed as untouchable authors, authors whom one cannot read or even cite in the field of political philosophy—and, *a fortiori*, in the field of critical theory—except as a foil, except as that *against which* our thinking takes shape, and that which we take as our project to undo. The neoliberal theorists are foreigners within our field of reference.

Indeed, neoliberal theory as a whole is largely conceived as dangerous and reactionary. Its principal authors are described as dubious characters or harmful ideologues who played decisive roles in the implementation of deregulatory policies and the disengagement of the welfare state. Responsibility for the advent of the "neoliberal society" is thus incumbent, in the final instance, upon the growing influence of this school of thought. For this reason, neoliberal theory is designated philosophical enemy number one. By violating the injunction that tells critical intellectuals to ignore or impugn this tradition as a matter of principle, Foucault challenged a deeply rooted reflex of leftist thought. This is why Foucault was perceived to have taken a turn to the right or, in any case, to have drifted away from traditional critical theory.

NEOLIBERALISM AS IDEOLOGY OF THE RIGHT

It is historically undeniable that most neoliberal authors were affiliated with the right, even with its most extreme wing. Numerous studies have attempted to show how the "conservative revolution" that befell the world at the end of the 1970s developed within exclusive circles where economists, intellectuals, engineers, and statesmen gathered to promote a radical neoliberalism.[1] The Walter Lippmann colloquium of 1938 and the Mont Pèlerin Society, created in 1947, have each been described as the first instances in which a concerted offensive against the achievements of Keynesianism was developed. Regulation of the economy, state interventionism, social protections, labor law, systems of collective assistance, wealth distribution, and so forth, were all called into question on behalf of the alleged moral and economic superiority of the free market. Moreover, some of the most celebrated neoliberal theoreticians—Friedrich Hayek and Milton Friedman most notably—instrumentally influenced the governments of Margaret Thatcher and Ronald Reagan.

Neoliberalism is thus generally regarded as a conservative doctrine. It is viewed as an ideology whose essential concern, whether in scholarly or philosophical form, is to further a reactionary politics. This view is rooted in the fact that, throughout the twentieth century, neoliberalism was elaborated within a framework dedicated to critiquing every form of leftist thought: Marxism, communism, socialism, Keynesianism, and, more generally, any ideology advocating the establishment of social-based policy.

Of course, liberal thought has always categorically rejected Marxism and attacked the totalitarian character of communist regimes. It affirms above all—and contrary to the position taken by many on the intellectual left—a direct link between Soviet and Chinese totalitarianism (and other totalitarian regimes) and Marxist the-

1. See Philip Mirowski and Dieter Plehwe, eds., *The Road From Mont Pèlerin: The Making of the Neoliberal Thought Collective* (Cambridge: Harvard University Press, 2009); and Gareth Steadman Jones, *Masters of the Universe: Hayek, Friedman, and the Birth of Neoliberal Politics* (Princeton: Princeton University Press, 2012).

ory. Liberals consistently reject the idea that these regimes should be viewed as "betrayals" of Marxism, as "deviations" or "errors" that do not invalidate the grandeur nor the relevance of the communist hypothesis. For liberals, these regimes applied the dogmas of the Marxist analysis to the letter. The failure of these historical experiences demonstrate not only the failure of communism as a political alternative to capitalism, but also the failure of Marxism as a theory and worldview articulated around a certain number of concepts (social classes, exploitation, surplus-value, alienation, etc.).

Yet this liberal perspective, such as it is, is not very original. It does not, in and of itself, explain the near unanimous rejection of the neoliberal tradition. We all know, for instance, that this view is not unique to liberals or even authors of the right. It is found in both non-Marxist socialists and in the anarchist tradition.

What is specific to the neoliberals is their dissatisfaction with resting on these denunciations alone. By building upon this critique of communism and the liberal rejection of Marxism, the neoliberals developed a much more radical posture. They sought to depart from the problems posed by communist regimes in order to develop an uncompromising analysis of Western democracies and the tendencies animating them. For the neoliberals, the authoritarian and totalitarian regimes everybody agrees to condemn should not be viewed as exceptional experiences that, as it were, do not concern us—or that only concern us as either objects of study or the subject of shared indignation. These regimes are much closer to us than we think. In fact, they flow logically from a banal and widely accepted ideological disposition common to all democratic societies: a distrust of the free market. Communism is merely one, albeit an extreme, ideology advocating control over the production and distribution of goods, or advocating an increase in state intervention in the economy in the name of "moral" values (justice, equity, etc.).

The clearest elaboration of the neoliberal view that any and all measures that impose greater regulation over the market (in order to ensure a more just allocation of resources) are potentially totalitarian is found in Austrian economist Friedrich Hayek's famous 1944 text, *The Road to Serfdom*.[2] Hayek's sole concern in this foundational book is to question the spontaneously accepted idea that what occurred in Russia in the 1920s and in Germany in the 1930s (Hayek, like most liberal thinkers, makes no fundamental distinction between the two) are the consequences of rare and unrepeatable circumstances. According to Hayek, conceiving communism and Nazism as aberrant experiences, and thereby positing a kind of incommensurability between totalitarianism on the one hand and English and American democracy on the other, prevents us from understanding the extent to which the analysis of these authoritarian regimes, and their emergence, tells us much about our own societies.

This type of analysis, according to Hayek, begins from the following premise: totalitarianism did not impose itself in Germany or in Russia suddenly or by chance. Rather, it was the end product of a gradual process, and it can absolutely repeat itself among us. If we wish to avoid the same tragedies, we must learn their lessons. To confront the question of totalitarianism thus compels us to rethink our politics, our state, our laws, our economic system, and so forth.

Hayek's core thesis is that the root of totalitarianism is located in the rejection of liberalism. The critique of individualism, the triumph of a collective ethic, the desire to substitute the play of the free and decentralized market for an institutional authority controlling the production and redistribution of wealth, all these elements constitute the point of departure, or better, the doctrinal basis of communism and National Socialism. Whenever these dogmas begin to spread, whenever they are adopted by the state, and whenever intellectuals legitimate them, totalitarianism is not far off; slowly but surely, and often unaware, we begin to travel down the road to serfdom.

At base, Hayek's masterstroke—and that of neoliberalism more generally—was to use these types of analyses to proffer the extremely powerful but disturbing thesis that there is something like a family resemblance, a contiguity of thought, or even a necessary

---

2. Friedrich Hayek, *The Road to Serfdom* (Chicago: University of Chicago Press, 2007).

relationship between not only communism and Nazism, but between communism and Keynesianism. Communist regimes, the Nazi regime, and any regime promoting social regulation and the welfare state all participate in the same system and belong to the same politico-economic variant. They all begin from the same refusal of liberalism, individualism, the free market, and decentralization, and—proceeding logically from this—they share the same willingness to use coercion to attain predefined goals in production and distribution. Consequently, and contrary to what we spontaneously imagine, totalitarianism is not something of the past. Totalitarians are among us: they are those who set up planning systems and those who justify social security, they are those who extol control over the economy by the state, they are those who advocate for market regulations, and they are who propose more taxes, and so forth.

Through this discourse, the neoliberal theorists attempted to reorient the cleavages that structure and define intellectual and political space. They introduced new systems of classification and new systems of vision and division. This is why neoliberalism should be viewed as an original and innovative theory. As Michel Foucault shows, the neoliberals challenged the pertinence of the traditional distinction between "socialism" and "capitalism." Whereas Keynesian regulatory policies were usually classified as forms of "capitalism" (a regulated capitalism), the neoliberals argued that these policies in fact share the same intent and inspiration as socialism. For liberals, then, the real opposition is not between "socialism" and "capitalism" but between "liberal" and "illiberal": on the one side of this divide there are those who adhere to the values of individualism and the free and decentralized market, and on the other side there are those—from the Nazis to the communists, and including all social reformers and partisans of the welfare state—who, each in their own way, advocate a collectivist ethic.

WHAT NEOLIBERALISM PRODUCES

The association—or rather the spontaneous reduction—of neoliberalism to this type of extremely ideological and even politically violent analysis explains the outright rejection this tradition usually meets. Given our normative frames of reference, there is something immediately incongruous, or even unacceptable, in the very idea of establishing a link between traditionally progressive policies on the one hand—such as the welfare state, unemployment insurance, welfare, equitable wealth distribution—and authoritarian or totalitarian regimes on the other. This discursive strategy has undoubtedly contributed to the muted reception of neoliberal doctrine as a whole. In other words, it seems as if the political affinities of the principal neoliberal authors have clouded the reception of their texts and hindered our ability to perceive divergent potentialities inscribed in their work. Instead of receiving their work as contributions to intellectual debate, their texts have been cataloged as simple ideological products animated by fundamentally reactionary, if not extremist, intentions.

Foucault's great audacity—and that which explains the continual miscomprehension of his texts on this subject—is to have parted with this common reception of neoliberalism and thereby broken through the symbolic barrier erected between the neoliberal tradition and the intellectual left—especially the so-called radical left. The project Foucault undertook was to read the principle theoreticians of neoliberalism, which is to say those who endowed the paradigm with its most radical expressions (such as Friedrich Hayek, Milton Friedman, and Gary Becker) in order to explore their representation of the world. He wanted to reconstitute neoliberalism's operational logic and the implicit hypotheses upon which it rests.

Obviously, this type of attitude is not synonymous with a conversion to neoliberalism, despite the many spontaneous interpretations of Foucault's texts on this matter. Foucault does not discuss the system as a dogma whose recommendations should be accepted and whose programs should be followed. His intention is subtler. He wants to deploy neoliberalism as a test. He wants to use it as an instrument for critiquing both reality and thought. It is a question of listening to this tradition in order to analyze ourselves.

Because this doctrine effectively constitutes the "negative" of our habitual theoretical space, confronting it means, in a certain sense, confronting our own unconscious and confronting the limits of our thought. It forces us to interrogate that which we hold as self-evident and that which we unknowingly discard when we formulate our theses. In other words, Foucault is building a kind of experimental apparatus: by immersing himself in this intellectual universe, he partakes—and invites us to partake—in an experience of disorientation that opens up the possibility of thinking differently and re-signifying the concepts of political philosophy and critical (and classical) theory—such as the state, democracy, the market, freedom, the law, or sovereignty—with radical new meanings. This return of the theoretically repressed is meant to dislodge our thinking and incite new languages of observation. Neoliberalism offers Foucault an opportunity to imagine other ways of looking at reality. One could almost say that it functions as a kind of cognitive housekeeping that radically interrogates the conceptual categories and perceptions we unwittingly carry around with us inside our heads.

To be disturbed by Foucault's analysis of neoliberalism is to ignore the very logic of the critical attitude itself. By fixing *a priori* the contents or concepts of leftist thought, denunciations of Foucault's analysis are based on a dogmatic and rigid definition of what the left should be: any discourse deviating from this norm is automatically designated as rightist or treasonous. Yet if we were to proffer a definition of the left, would it not be based on the willingness to continually rethink ourselves? And if we were to characterize the critical gesture, would it not consist in continually re-examining what it means to critique?

THE CONDITIONS OF CRITIQUE

Constituting neoliberalism as an instrument for opening a pathway to self-reflection does not, of course, mean neoliberalism should be taken as a given, self-evident phenomenon whose reality and characteristics should be passively accepted. For Foucault, neoliberalism is not merely a jumping off point for critical self-interrogation: it is a doctrine that, naturally, must also be questioned. This is why Foucault insists on the fact that one of the central issues of *The Birth of Biopolitics* is the matter of addressing the conditions under which a genuine critique of neoliberal "governmentality" can be developed.

One of Foucault's principle objectives in this text is to liberate thought from its mantras, from the sloganeering statements sempiternally used to denounce the evils of neoliberalism, but which have long been used to undermine classical liberalism and even capitalism. There are, according to Foucault, a series of "analytical and critical frameworks . . . repeating the same type of critique for two hundred, one hundred or ten years"[3] : they accuse capitalism, liberalism, and now neoliberalism of creating a "mass society," a "society of one-dimensional man, of authority, of consumption, of the spectacle, and so forth."[4] Foucault speaks amusingly of those authors who repeat this same critique, who speak this anonymous discourse or—better yet—who are spoken by it. According to Foucault, these "commonplaces of thought whose articulation and framework we know very well" have circulated at least since the beginning of the twentieth century.[5] He cites the theses formulated by German sociologist Werner Sombart, between 1906 and 1934, as an exaggerated example that functions, in his text, something like a magnifying glass. Foucault summarizes Sombart's theses in these terms:

> What have the bourgeois and capitalist economy and state produced? They have produced a society in which individuals have been torn from their natural community and brought together in the flat, anonymous form of the mass. Capitalism produces the mass. Capitalism consequently produces what Sombart does not

---

3. Foucault, *The Birth of Biopolitics*, 130.
4. Ibid., 113–14.
5. Ibid., 113.

exactly call one-dimensionality, but this is precisely what he
defines. Capitalism and bourgeois society have deprived individuals of direct and immediate communication with each other and
they are forced to communicate through the intermediary of a
centralized administrative apparatus. [They have] therefore reduced individuals to the state of atoms subject to an abstract
authority in which they do not recognize themselves. Capitalist
society has also forced individuals into a type of mass consumption with the functions of standardization and normalization. Finally, this bourgeois and capitalist economy has doomed individuals to communicate with each other only through the play of
signs and spectacles. [6]

The idea that capitalism produces a utilitarian, individualistic world,
marked by the development of mass phenomenon, consumption,
and uniformity, was a common and even dominant trope amongst
the intellectual left—and even a certain fraction of the right. It has
been rehearsed to an almost obsessional degree, and the situation
today has hardly changed: nearly all the discourses hostile to neoliberalism repeat these same criticisms.

According to Foucault, we must immediately rid ourselves of the
analytical matrices "with which [the] problem of neoliberalism is
usually approached."[7] For these matrices are, in fact, only critical in
appearance: at base they are empty declarations devoid of any efficacy. Why? Because they ignore neoliberalism's singularity. These
traditional discourses assimilate neoliberalism into classical liberalism, classical liberalism into capitalism, capitalism into the domination of the bourgeoisie, and so forth, as if they were all the same
thing. They create a unifying and homogeneous grand narrative
from which nothing new can emerge. They "[coat] the present in a
form that is recognized in the past" and consider the present a "simple repetition" of the past.[8] They transpose older historical matrices
onto the present as if "what existed then is the same as what exists

---

6. Ibid.
7. Ibid., 130.
8. Ibid., 130–31.

now."[9] Consequently, they are condemned to miss their target: they obscure present reality instead of developing tools for understanding it and, therefore, challenging it.

It is precisely to avoid such biases that Foucault considers it essential to read the neoliberal theoreticians and understand what they are trying to do. The point of departure for the critical analysis of neoliberalism must be an apprehension of this phenomenon in its singularity: "what I would like to show you is precisely that neoliberalism is really something else. Whether it is of great significance or not, I don't know, but assuredly it is something, and I would like to try to grasp it in its singularity."[10]

The Birth of Biopolitics can thus be read as a meditation on critique, on what critique means and presupposes: the condition for formulating a practice of resistance to neoliberalism lies in revealing the specificity of this phenomenon. But why must we, in addition to this, also interrogate ourselves? Why does Foucault go even further and turn neoliberal theory into an instrument for renewing theory itself? Only this approach, in Foucault's view, makes it possible to challenge neoliberalism in a way that escapes nostalgia and doesn't oppose neoliberalism to that which it has already defeated.

We are thus dealing here with one of the central problems confronted by every great radical author: how do we defuse the backward-looking and reactionary potential necessarily inscribed in the heart of every critical project? How can we challenge the present order without this leading, almost automatically, to a veneration of the previous order, or to perceiving the present as a moment we can only lament? And thus, more specifically, how do we conceive a critical investigation of neoliberalism that does not valorize what neoliberalism defeated, and which does not, consciously or unconsciously, fall back onto pre-liberal values?

To avoid such difficulties, Foucault proposes thinking the historical rupture engendered by the emergence of neoliberal governmentality in terms of singularity and originality. That is to say, to think

---

9.   Ibid., 130.
10.   Ibid.

neoliberalism "positively": the novelty of neoliberalism must be discerned. We must break with the problematic of "loss," "destruction," and "grief" that structures the traditional discourse of neoliberalism and its history. We must cease asking ourselves what will "undo" these liberal logics as well as merely documenting that which they "destroy." It is necessary, on the contrary, to ask what they *produce*. We must not simply lament that which has emerged as a result of neoliberalism but, on the contrary, we must begin to ask what neoliberalism is so we can better determine what it compels us to reconsider.

Foucault thus intends to renew theory by giving it the means to reconcile a positive perception of neoliberalism's singularity with its radical critique. It is worth noting, in this sense, that Foucault's gesture is very similar to Marx's 1875 critique of the German socialists' account of capitalism. One of the central points in Marx's *Critique of the Gotha Program* is his reproach against the social democrats for conceiving the bourgeoisie as part of a great "reactionary" class—in which we also find members of the middle and "feudal" classes—whom the "workers" must oppose. According to Marx, such a diagnosis is absurd. It completely misses the singularity of the economic and social situation of the late nineteenth century. For Marx, grasping the "positivity" of capitalism is to understand and accept the bourgeoisie as an authentically revolutionary class: the bourgeoisie has transformed economic relations and emancipated individuals from their traditional roots; it substituted relations of feudal subjugation for juridical relations between formally "equal" men and the mutual exchange of goods and services through the market. In Marx's view, we cannot approach the problem of the bourgeoisie in negative terms—especially if the objective is to struggle against the bourgeoisie itself. Otherwise, we are condemned, like the social democrats, to confuse revolution and reaction—that is to say, to proffer as revolutionary a restorative politics that re-establishes realities the bourgeoisie have defeated and rendered obsolete. This is what Marx calls the "pre-capitalist critique of capitalism."[11] To avoid such impasses, Marx affirms the necessity of approaching the bourgeoisie and capitalism as revolutionary phenomena. We must grasp their contributions positively: what have they produced? What have they invented in terms of new rights, new freedoms, and new forms of emancipation? What new realities have they imposed upon our existence? In a sense, communism, as Marx defined it in several of his texts, appears as a means of realizing a certain number of emancipatory ideals that were promised by the bourgeois revolution but which it did not succeed in implementing, and which it even actively prevented by re-establishing a market-based system of collective exploitation (class relations). The communist revolution is not, therefore, defined as a reaction against the bourgeois revolution. In a certain sense, it is part of its heritage and even strives to radicalize it; that is to say, it begins from what the bourgeoisie invented in order to reactivate and regenerate—and thus transform it totally.

Foucault approaches, and invites us to approach, neoliberalism in the same spirit. He formulates the same analytical principles and employs the same mode of problematization. For the author of *The History of Sexuality*, a critical history of neoliberalism must reveal what is being invented through neoliberalism and what new types of politico-economic arrangements, concepts, and representations it compels us to take into account. Neoliberalism created new conceptions of the state, the market, and the ownership of oneself and one's body. It has created new democratic, social, and cultural demands, and ushered in new relationships of violence, morality, and diversity. It challenges the legitimacy of any number of traditional systems of regulation and control. To put oneself in contact with this new tradition is thus to give oneself the means to reveal, at the same time and in the same movement, the promise of emancipation embodied in neoliberalism *and* the reasons why it has not fulfilled such promises. It is to search, within the internal contradictions traversing and undermining neoliberalism, for zones that are vulnerable to

---

11. Karl Marx, "Critique of the Gotha Program." In *Marx-Engels Reader*, edited by Robert C. Tucker (New York: W.W. Norton, 1978).

transformative politics while still retaining and taking up its most valuable and legitimate demands. This is in stark contrast to those discourses that myopically focus on the dangers arising from this new situation and which end up offering a return to the past as the only possible political horizon.

I

NEOLIBERALISM AS UTOPIA

It is impossible to understand Foucault's interest in neoliberalism, which indeed resembles a kind of fascination at times, without recognizing his intent to break with the habit of reading neoliberalism as a conservative or reactionary ideology. One of the more prominent tendencies in the media and in political and intellectual literature is to portray the perpetuation of order as one of neoliberalism's fundamental characteristics. Neoliberalism, according to this view, is a doctrine permanently opposed to change and which continually strives to preserve the prevailing order.

This conservative conceptualization of neoliberalism is manifest in the critique, by neoliberal partisans, of all the utopias that call for the establishment of organizations alternative to the market society. By denouncing socialism, communism, etc., neoliberalism forecloses the possibility of imagining other societal models. Neoliberalism does not incite rebellion but rather resignation and the acceptance of the present situation. And more seriously, neoliberal dogmas stand in the way of anything that might upset the established operation of the market economy: neoliberal doctrine questions the validity of even the smallest reforms designed to produce a greater redistribution of wealth. In other words, neoliberalism stands resolutely on the side of the status quo. It is the embodiment of one of the principle forces that resist change. It represents the ideology of the ruling class, which is to the say the class whose interest it is to perpetuate the present situation as it is.

This conservative perception of neoliberalism is both deeply entrenched and structures much of the critical rhetoric on neoliberalism. And yet it is based on a profound misunderstanding of this tradition. Indeed, this view does much to obscure any real comprehension of neoliberalism: it neutralizes it by reducing it to the familiar. Rather than confronting neoliberalism's specificity, this discourse reduces neoliberalism to something easy to fight and denounce.

Since the end of the Second World War, however, and especially during the 1960s, one of the central preoccupations of the neoliberals was to distinguish themselves from conservatism. Liberals and conservatives have, of course, formed alliances in the past and sometimes find themselves taking up identical positions. But this is only because they share common enemies (socialists and supporters of the welfare state). As Friedrich Hayek argued in a famous article, "Why I am not a Conservative":

> At a time when most movements that are thought to be progressive advocate further encroachments on individual liberty, those who cherish freedom are likely to expend their energies in opposition. In this they find themselves much of the time on the same side as those who habitually resist change. In matters of current politics today they generally have little choice but to support the conservative parties.[1]

But according to Hayek (and many other writers who defend this same view) the proximity between liberals and conservatives ends here. It is purely political—or more accurately, it is strategic and temporary. It is rooted in a shared motivation to block progressive movements. It is a negative alliance, and it should not mask the profound points of divergence separating neoliberalism from conservatism.

---

1. Friedrich Hayek, "Why I am Not a Conservative." In *The Constitution of Liberty* (Chicago: University of Chicago Press, 1960), 88.

From the perspective of the history of ideas, this relationship is very important: for it constitutes perhaps the essential point of rupture between neoliberalism and classical liberalism. It marks the birth of neoliberalism as a doctrine that is distinct, singular, and irreducible to that which preceded it. The neoliberals never cease to affirm, and denounce, the fact that their predecessors have been corrupted by conservatism. They are too close to the conservative right—even the reactionary right—to the point of only marginal differentiation.[2] Satisfied that many of their demands had triumphed by the mid-nineteenth century, the classical liberals gradually withdrew and seemed content to merely defend the existing order. Classical liberalism thus gradually ceased to be a radical movement. It was transformed into a machine for preserving the status quo. Liberalism was now situated on the side of order, with the powers that be. It opposed revolutionary doctrines and any aspirations for change. It styled itself the guarantor of realism or rational politics.[3]

By adopting this posture, however, the liberals betrayed themselves. They considerably weakened their position and left the door open for the success of their socialist enemies: by abandoning the terrain of intellectual speculation and political imagination, classical liberalism was no longer capable of arousing enthusiasm, and no longer seemed to propose ideas that were worth fighting for. Contrarily, the socialists were now afforded the opportunity to appear to be the only rebels, the only authentic protestors. They proposed another path, another program, another vision. This is why their numbers swelled, especially among intellectuals and students: "for over half a century it has been only the socialists who have offered anything like an explicit program of social development, a picture of the future society at which they were aiming, and a set of general principles to guide decisions on particular issues."[4]

---

2. For more on this question, see the very knowledgeable and helpful book by Sébastien Caré, *La Pensée libertarienne* (Paris: PUF, 2009), 8–18 in particular.

3. See Friedrich Hayek, "The Intellectuals and Socialism." In *Studies in Philosophy, Politics and Economics* (London: Routledge & Kegan Paul, 1967).

4. Hayek, "The Intellectuals and Socialism," 190.

The neoliberal thinkers wanted to tear down this partition, this division established between conservative liberalism on the one side and reformative socialism on the other, between the party of immobility and the party of movement. Unlike the classical liberals, the neoliberals contested socialism's monopoly over the production of political and philosophical utopias. They want to make their doctrine a radical, even revolutionary, doctrine. It is thus no coincidence that one of the major books of the neoliberal tradition in its more extreme version—Robert Nozick's *Anarchy, State, and Utopia* (1974)—sought to reanimate liberalism's original powers of destabilization. Similarly, Hayek evoked the necessity of creating what he referred to as a "liberal utopia" as early as 1949:

> What we lack is a liberal utopia, a program which seems neither a mere defense of things as they are nor a diluted kind of socialism, but a truly liberal radicalism which does not spare the susceptibilities of the mighty (including the trade unions), which is not too severely practical, and which does not confine itself to what appears today as politically possible.[5]

Understanding neoliberalism means conceptualizing its doctrine as something more than an economic or social reality endowed with materiality and objectivity. Neoliberalism is a project, an ambition that is never completed and that needs to be perpetually reactivated. It must be grasped as something on the order of an "aspiration." Foucault, in fact, goes even further and defines neoliberalism as a kind of ethics, a "many-sided, ambiguous, global claim with a foothold in both the left and the right."[6] It is not a political alternative structured by a well-defined program or plan. It is something much more diffuse: it is a disposition, a "utopian focus," or a "general style of thought, analysis and imagination."[7]

5. Ibid., 194.
6. Foucault, *The Birth of Biopolitics*, 218.
7. Ibid., 218–19.

2

THE MARKET EVERYWHERE

What is the nature of the neoliberal utopia? What transformative actions do its authors intend to carry out? What vision of society do they promote? At first glance, this seems rather straightforward: the essence of the neoliberal project is to institute a thoroughgoing commodification of society. For the neoliberal theorists, the objective is clear: the only valid form of social organization is the market. Contract and exchange between individuals must be valorized over and against all other types of human relationships and against alternative modes of resource allocation.

This market utopia, this ambition to spread the market everywhere, is one of the reasons why we cannot conceive of the relationship between classical liberalism (Smith, Ricardo, Say) and neoliberalism in terms of continuity or linearity. On this point, there is definite rupture and discontinuity between the two traditions: each offers distinctive conceptions of the market and its place in society—and, more importantly, between economic rationality and the state.

Eighteenth-century classical liberalism, whose principle representative was Adam Smith, developed according to the watchword "laissez-faire." Laissez-faire denoted restricting state interventionism and fixing a certain number of limits in order to create a "free" space in which market mechanisms could function without external constraint. According to liberal governmentality, we find the market and economic rationality on the one side, and the state and political rationality on the other. The point at issue, for classical liberalism, is to tell the state: "beyond such and such a limit, regarding such and such a question, and starting at the borders of such and such a domain, you will no longer intervene."[1]

Neoliberalism is very different, however, and its project is much more radical. Foucault articulates its characteristics through a discussion of two traditions: German postwar ordo-liberalism, which was concentrated around the journal *Ordo* (Walter Eucken, Franz Böhm, etc.) and the Chicago School economists (Ludwig von Mises, Milton Friedman, Gary Becker, etc.). According to Foucault, these traditions have no intention of preserving a specific and proper space for the market, which then co-exists alongside other rationalities, especially that of the state. On the contrary, their goal is to *spread the market everywhere*. The mechanisms of competition should not be limited to certain sectors. They must be extended to the whole of society. They must play their regulatory role as widely as possible and across as many domains of social life as possible. The neoliberal utopia, in short, is to absorb our entire reality within the ambit of the market.

This ambition to sublimate the law of the market for the law proper, and to submit all aspects of social life to the laws of the market, explains why neoliberalism is at odds with the classical doctrine of laissez-faire. In order to be realized, the neoliberal utopia presupposes the establishment of an expansive system of political and legal interventionism. As Foucault describes it, "neo-liberal governmental intervention is no less dense, frequent, active, and continuous than in any other system."[2] But this interventionism is unique in that it is not at all intended to "correct" the market; it does not try to contrast economic rationality with some other social or political rationality, nor does it impede the normal operation of competition by invoking ethical, moral, or social justice–oriented

---

1. Foucault, *The Birth of Biopolitics*, 116.
2. Ibid., 145.

demands. On the contrary, this interventionism functions in the service of the market form, and it works in order to develop and generalize the institution of the market. Neoliberalism wants to transform society according to a veritable "politics of competition" that disseminates the market form everywhere:

> [Neoliberal governmentality] has to intervene on society as such, in its fabric and depth. Basically, it has to intervene on society so that competitive mechanisms can play a regulatory role at every moment and every point in society and by intervening in this way its objective will become possible, that is to say, a general regulation of society by the market.[3]

This project obviously affects every sector of the social world, but it affects the state first and foremost. Classical liberalism preserved a boundary between economics and politics, thus enabling the peaceful coexistence between a market rationality and a political rationality (as long as each remains in its proper place). Neoliberalism, inversely, submits political rationality (along with every other domain of society) to the imperatives of economic rationality. The state is placed under the surveillance of the market. It must not only legislate in the interest of the market, but it must, itself, function according to a market logic:

> The problem of neo-liberalism was not how to cut out or contrive a free space of the market within an already given political society, as in the liberalism of Adam Smith and the eighteenth-century. The problem of neo-liberalism is rather how the overall exercise of political power can be modeled on the principles of a market economy.[4]

According to Foucault, this system is absolutely unique because, here, the legitimacy of the state and its actions are not the result of its own autonomous principles. The economy is now the basis of

---

3. Ibid., 145.
4. Ibid., 131.

politics and it determines the form and character of public intervention.

3

THE "SCIENTIFIC" JUSTIFICATION
FOR THE MARKET

In many respects, the principal reason neoliberal thinking arouses such hostility is its strict adherence to the market form, its desire to diffuse, institute, and apply the market form to all domains of social life. In short, it is due to its rather extreme conception of a society in which a competitive logic and a market rationality reigns completely. Evoking this aspect of neoliberalism alone is usually sufficient to provoke indignant reactions and even a kind of dread.

Hostility toward the "market" is, of course, extremely widespread. In our collective unconscious—especially for the left—the market is a profoundly suspect term. So much so, in fact, that one of the most widely employed polemical instruments used to discredit or disqualify an idea, claim, or reform is to suggest it partakes in a "market logic," which is to say a neoliberal logic. And often such claims are made without understanding very well why the "logic of the market" conjures up such a negative reality.

Theorizing neoliberalism positively is thus contingent on overcoming this reflex. It demands a more nuanced interrogation of why the neoliberal intellectuals are so attached to the market form: *why* do they make this particular mode of organization the only possible or, more accurately, the only valid form of social organization? What is it about the market, in their eyes, that makes it so valuable, even irreplaceable, such that it must be extended to the whole of society and govern every possible sector?

It would of course be easy to answer this question by saying the market is simply an instrument of economic exploitation, and the neoliberals are its partisan advocates. From this perspective, neoliberal theory appears as nothing more than the ideology of the ruling class and, ultimately, the neoliberals praise the market in order to defend—or even augment—the privileges accrued by those who have an interest in perpetuating the current system.[1]

This depiction is not, however, very illuminating. In the first instance, this view too crudely identifies neoliberal theory with contemporary economic and social interests. It is a reductive (and banal) interpretation of a tradition that, we must not forget, has made important contributions to debates in the fields of sociology, economics, philosophy, etc. The entire conceptual dimension of neoliberalism disappears once it is depicted as merely a class-based economic doctrine.

But above all, positing the market as the ideology of the ruling class is to read the neoliberal theoreticians as belonging to a theoretical system they actually defined themselves *against*. It is to look at them from an external point of view. It is to apply categories to the neoliberals they themselves attempted to undo. Obviously, such an approach is not, *a priori*, illegitimate, but it does nonetheless prevent us from understanding the singularity of this paradigm, the new types of problems that it poses, and the new ways in which it poses them. Foucault, inversely, tries to put himself in the place of these authors in order to grasp their particular vision of the world.

Foucault evokes, of course, the most essential, well-known, and widespread manner in which the neoliberals justify the market and the assertion that competitive mechanisms should be inscribed within the very heart of society. This foundational argument is generally presented as technical in nature, and it has been formulated by different schools of economic thought: the Austrian School (Carl Men-

---

1. See, for instance, David Harvey, *A Brief History of Neoliberalism* (Oxford: Oxford University Press, 2005).

ger, Ludwig von Mises, and Friedrich Hayek) but also the Marginal-
ist School (Leon Walras, William Stanley Jevon, and Alfred Mar-
shall). This argument relies upon economistic reasoning that affirms
the market as the most efficient mechanism for allocating resources.
Every other mode of production and distribution proves, sooner or
later, to be less efficient than the market: communism, interventionism, state planning, monopoly, etc. Any economic system that im-
pedes decentralized market mechanisms and the natural adjustment
of prices in response to supply and demand necessarily results in a
net loss. It leads to the destruction of collective wealth and de-
creases private and social well-being, compared to what could have
been achieved through competitive equilibrium (a few exceptional
and local cases aside). The market is thus articulated as one technique of economic coordination among others, but it is the one that
happens to be the most efficient. In her summary of Hayek's work,
for instance, Catherine Audard writes:

> Hayek is undoubtedly the modern thinker who best understood
> communism's inability to compete with capitalism as not stem-
> ming from its moral inferiority, but from the fact that it is less
> efficient because it doesn't understand the nature of economic
> processes. It is not the engineer, but the entrepreneur who is best
> positioned to grasp economic processes, because the entrepren-
> eur understands the economy from the "inside," by continually
> receiving all the necessary information through the market and
> the pricing system.[2]

It is of course easy to understand why the neoliberals would proffer
this type of argument: it endows their politics with an air of scientific authority. The entire discussion proceeds as if the debate about
the market revolves around a purely technical question. It is simply
a matter of objectively evaluating the relative efficiency of different
economic systems. Neoliberalism, contrary to appearances and what
is generally written on the subject, is not therefore an ideology: it is

---

2. Catherine Audard, *Qu'est-ce que le libéralisme?* (Paris: Gallimard, 2009), 374–75.

scientifically grounded, and one can do nothing more than bow before the implacable logic of its mathematical rationality.

In many respects, then, rhetorically constructing neoliberal discourse as a form of scientific argumentation is a strategic operation deployed by the neoliberal theoreticians. It is a means of exerting intimidation: this doctrine has science on its side, and alternative theories must accept the facts. And perhaps it is also a means of dampening the polemical character of the debate, of undermining the violent response neoliberal writings often provoked by framing the issue as nothing more than a matter of calmly comparing the relative optimality of different mechanisms for allocating resources.

Foucault does not spend much time discussing this aspect of neoliberal rationality in *The Birth of Biopolitics*. He is more interested in thinking about the manner in which reflection on the market form resonates with a whole series of political, ethical, and philosophical issues. It should be noted, however, that contrasting "technical" or "economic" considerations against "theoretical" concerns misses the point. For one of the specificities of neoliberalism is its ability to render these otherwise distinctive registers inseparable and inextricably linked to each other: for it is precisely by posing problems in technical terms that the neoliberal authors begin to encounter political, social, and ethical dilemmas. It is almost as if the inevitable logic of economic reasoning eventually propels those who wield it beyond the borders of the economic as such. Consequently, what is at stake in neoliberalism, from the point of view of social theory or political philosophy, is inherent in the same system, or the same apparatus, as that which is at stake in the merely "scientific" approach to economic policy. We are dealing with two sides of the same coin. It is thus no coincidence that the work of the author who has probably gone farthest in defending neoliberalism on the grounds of efficiency—namely, Friedrich Hayek—is where we also find the most innovative and radical theoretical advances in the entire field of neoliberal theory—with perhaps the exception of the work of economist Gary Becker.

4

ON PLURALITY

The traditional understanding of neoliberal philosophy rests upon the idea that neoliberalism is a doctrine whose principle value is freedom—alongside private property and natural law. Neoliberalism, in this view, is determined to defend the sovereignty of the individual, both in terms of private property and one's person. Of course this defense takes different forms and is deployed with varying degrees of vigor and radicalism, but every version of neoliberalism inscribed within this common conceptual framework fully and completely ascribes to the principle that every individual should be free to use their possessions as they see fit, while denouncing as illegitimate any action aimed at restricting this use. The notion of "freedom" then, for both liberalism and neoliberalism, is the privileged instrument of their radical critique: it is deployed against any instance in which, in their view, individual property rights are violated—particularly by the state, whose social and economic interventionism necessarily leads to the multiplication of coercive mechanisms (taxes, regulations, etc.). The defense of the market is thus inscribed within a more general defense of freedom. In fact, the neoliberals have always articulated economic freedom as no less important than any other political freedom.[1]

To support this view, one need only recall the fact that many of the great works in the liberal tradition pay homage to the value of freedom in their very titles: *On Liberty* by John Stuart Mill, Isaiah Berlin's collection of essays,[2] *The Constitution of Liberty* by Friedrich Hayek, and *The Ethics of Liberty* by Murray Rothbard, one of the central theoreticians of libertarianism and anarcho-capitalism.

Foucault contests this dominant view of neoliberalism by offering an alternative vision of this tradition, one that relativizes the importance of freedom—and, accordingly, natural rights—within neoliberal thought. Specifically, he suggests the central concept of the neoliberal paradigm is not freedom but rather *plurality*. Whereas the concept of freedom still fulfills an important role in neoliberal thought, it often plays a subordinate or secondary role in relation to the notion of plurality. In other words, neoliberalism must be conceived as a meditation on multiplicity and an attempt to theorize a society that adopts plurality as its central theme. What is unique about this paradigm, then, is that it forces us to ask ourselves what it might mean to live in a society composed of individuals or groups who experiment with diverse modes of life.

This framework makes it possible to understand the importance that neoliberal thought attaches to the market form. According to the neoliberals, the market is the only mode of regulation that is compatible with the essential features of contemporary society: specifically, its fundamentally diverse economics and its pluralistic modes of life. Or, even better, one could say that as soon as one sides with diversity, plurality, social innovation, etc., the logic of the market is preferable to every other mode of organization, especially the logic of the state.

---

1. See, for example, Milton Freidman, "The Relationship between Economic Freedom and Political Freedom." In *Capitalism and Freedom* (Chicago: University of Chicago Press, 2002).
2. Isaiah Berlin, *Freedom and its Betrayal: Six Enemies of Human Liberty* (Princeton, NJ: Princeton University Press, 2014); and *Four Essays on Liberty* (Oxford: Oxford University Press, 2002).

This is precisely the argument made by Friedrich Hayek. For Hayek, the fundamental characteristic of modern society is heterogeneity. Industrialization produced a massive shift in the traditional division of labor, and new businesses proliferated as a result of increasing specialization. Contemporary societies are thus far more differentiated than their pre-modern counterparts and, consequently, centralized administration of the economy becomes impossible:

> There would be no difficulty about efficient control or planning were conditions so simple that a single person or board could effectively survey all the relevant facts. It is only as the factors which have to be taken into account become so numerous that it is impossible to gain a synoptic view of them that decentralization becomes imperative.[3]

State administration claims to supplant the market on behalf of the general interest, the common good, social well-being, etc. But what meanings do such values have in a diverse world? How does one conceive of a "collective" plan agreed to by each individual? How can one claim to have arrived at a complete and universally valid moral code, or pursue a course assented by all? "It would be impossible for any mind to comprehend the infinite variety of different needs of different people which compete for available resources and attach a definite weight to each."[4] This fundamental impossibility of gaining "total" knowledge, of building a unified vision of society, explains why the only possible posture is to reject all forms of centralized control and promote the logic of the market. Only a market logic leaves individuals to their own devices and refrains from directing their actions. Neoliberal philosophy, Hayek concludes, is thus based on

> the indisputable fact that the limits of our powers of imagination make it impossible to include in our scale of values more than a sector of the needs of the whole society, and that, since, strictly

---

3. Friedrich Hayek, *The Road to Serfdom* (Chicago: University of Chicago Press, 1944), 48–49.
4. Ibid., 58.

speaking, scales of value can exist only in individual minds,
nothing but partial scales of values exist—scales which are inev-
itably different and often inconsistent with each other.[5]

And this is ultimately why "individuals should be allowed, within
defined limits, to follow their own values and preferences rather
than somebody else's. Within these spheres, the individual's system
of ends should be supreme and not subject to any dictation by others."[6]

---

5. Ibid., 59.
6. Ibid.

5

SOCIETY, COMMUNITY, UNITY

By affirming "diversity" and "multiplicity" as privileged social values, and by committing to a policy of inventing permanent apparatuses for the protection and proliferation of difference, neoliberalism pursues a very precise theoretical project. It wants to break with every intellectual tradition that strives to build a "monistic" vision of the social world. In this sense, the principal enemy of neoliberalism is not, as it is often believed, socialism, Marxism, or interventionist and collectivist programs more generally. These doctrines have undoubtedly been subject to some of neoliberalism's fiercest attacks, but the ceaseless polemics against anti-capitalist traditions actually obscure our understanding of neoliberal thought.

What neoliberalism opposes with the most force and consistency is a more general philosophical attitude at work across different traditions, countries, and historical periods, but which, according to its proponents, finds its original genesis in Enlightenment thought. It is an attitude promoting a unified or unifying conception of society by valorizing everything pertaining to the "common," the "collective," or the "general," to the detriment of the "individual," the "particular," or the "local."

For the neoliberals, traditional political philosophy is driven by an authoritarian and conservative impulse. Political philosophy has systematically constructed a theory of political sovereignty and law in order to deal with its preoccupying concern with plurality and diversity. In order for society to be "possible," in order to constitute a "body politic" worthy of the name, traditional political philosophy has deemed it necessary to invent apparatuses that regulate and manage social plurality. Order, unity, and collectivity are only possible if modes of life are limited in their multiplicity. In short, social theory, according to the neoliberals, is always totalizing. It cannot conceive of a genuinely plural society.

Paradoxically, it is the philosophers of the contract—from Rousseau to Rawls (and passing through Kant)—who best illustrate this posture. These theorists conceive of the "problem" of social order in a very specific way; better, it is precisely that they conceive of social order as a "problem" in the first place. They begin with the existence of different individuals leading separate lives and harboring potentially conflicting interests. And from this premise a dilemma immediately arises: how is social cooperation possible? How can we establish something like a "society" endowed with some measure of coherence? The "social contract" is the name given to the institution tasked with unifying society and soliciting the emergence of the "general" out of a framework of seemingly irreducible "particular" interests.

In this sense, then, the neoliberal theorists formulate a thoroughgoing reinterpretation of the philosophy of the contract and the Enlightenment. This tradition is often associated with the struggle against ethnic, racial, or cultural particularism. It affirms the superiority of the universal over the influence of local affiliation, and all on behalf of values such as personal autonomy, individual liberty, and formal equality. In reality, however, the neoliberals see Enlightenment thought as another means of establishing community. Enlightenment thought liberates individuals from natural communities only to more effectively subject them to a new type of collective: the political community.

To demonstrate this, the neoliberals deconstruct the central concept of the Enlightenment paradigm: *autonomy*. What does it mean for Enlightenment thought, and for Rousseau and Kant in particular, to be autonomous? It is not simply to be independent or unhindered (in accordance with the liberal conception freedom provided by Isaiah Berlin as simple non-interference or "negative liberty"). In fact, being autonomous means denying one's own instincts, passions, or natural inclinations. Autonomy is the "successful self-detachment from . . . forces for which I am not in any case responsible."[1] In this context, "freedom" is conceived as the act of "issuing orders to myself which I, being free to do as I will, obey."[2] In other words, the Enlightenment subject does not like choice for the sake of choice, or choice *per se*: rather, this subject is always searching for the *right* choice. The subject is free if and only if it obeys its own "true" law, or follows its own "true will" (this is the concept of "positive liberty"). The political community is thus conceived as the institution in which this superior law is established, and which every rational subject should recognize as their own. In the words of Isaiah Berlin, "individual self-determination now becomes collective self-realization, and the nation [becomes] a community of unified wills in pursuit of moral truths."[3] There is thus a principled affinity between Enlightenment thought and the notion of community, insofar as freedom, once filtered through the concept of autonomy, is conceived as willful submission to the nation.

Rousseau's analysis in *The Social Contract* (1762) is a famous example of this. It presupposes a condition in which men confront obstacles hindering their preservation: the primitive state or the state of nature, in which individuals mature in isolation, is no longer viable. It endangers both the species and the survival of each individual. This is why men are compelled to unite and why it becomes necessary to constitute a people. And for Rousseau, constituting a people means abandoning this prior condition of isolated individuality in favor of "community." What the social contract is all about, then, is showing how the condition upon which a political commu-

---

1.   Isaiah Berlin, *Freedom and Its Betrayal* (Princeton: Princeton University Press, 2002), 65–66.

2.   Ibid., 66. On the opposition between "negative liberty" and "positive liberty" see, from the same author, *Four Essays on Liberty* (Oxford: Oxford University Press, 2002). One could further consult the work of Quentin Skinner, most notably *Liberty Before Liberalism* (Cambridge: Cambridge University Press, 1998).

3.   Berlin, *Freedom and its Betrayal*, 74.

nity is constituted is the repression of variation. The social contract is not, strictly speaking, a contract: it is the name, given by Rousseau, to the moment in which individuals renounce their particularity or partiality—that is to say that which separates and distinguishes them from each other—in order to reconstitute themselves as "moral" or "communitarian" individuals who adopt the general will as their own. A social body is thus only possible or even conceivable at that moment in which some new framework arrives and replaces the law of individuality for the law of the community. The emergence of a people presupposes a foundational act through which the "general interest" and the "general will" eradicate the play of particular interests:[4]

> If therefore we set aside everything that is not essential to the social pact, we shall find that it may be reduced to the following terms. Each of us puts [their] person and all [their] power under the supreme direction of the general will, and we as a body receive each member as an indivisible part of the whole. Immediately, this act of association produces, in place of the individual persons of every contracting party, a moral and collective body, which is comprised of as many members as there are votes in the assembly, and which, by the same act, is endowed with its unity, its common self, its life and its will. The public person that is formed in this way by the union of all the others once bore the name *city*, and now bears that of *republic* or *body politic*; its members call it *the state* when it is passive, *the sovereign* when it is active, and a *power* when comparing it to its like. As regards the associates, they collectively take the name of *people*, and are individually called *citizens* as being participants in sovereign authority, and *subjects* as being bound by the laws of the state.[5]

We can clearly see in this passage how Rousseau's rhetoric, his conception of the politico-social order, and his idea of what makes

---

4.   See Louis Althusser, *Politique et histoire* (Paris: Seuil, 2006).
5.   Jean-Jacques Rousseau, *The Social Contract*, translated by Christopher Betts (Oxford: Oxford University Press, 1994), 55–56. Also see Ernst Cassirer, *The Question of Jean-Jacques Rousseau* (New Haven: Yale University Press, 1989).

society worthy of its name is everywhere preoccupied with the themes of unity, community, and generality, over and against notions of diversity and plurality.

This conception of society as a body whose formation presupposes "that on one occasion at least there has been unanimity"[6]— which is to say agreement and consensus—and which is imagined as a supra-individual entity destined to unify particular consciousnesses, is found in almost identical terms in Kant. The construction of a "people," as Kant asserts in *The Metaphysics of Morals*, presupposes the establishment of a "constitution" designed to "unify" an "aggregation" of men. Kant's commonwealth is thus conceived, once again, as an act of unification establishing the reign of "common interests" over and against the particular interests of individuals: "a state is a union of an aggregation of men under rightful laws."[7] Kant follows this assertion with a particularly explicit passage on this point:

> *Public right* is the sum total of laws which require to be made universally public in order to produce a state of right. It is therefore a system of laws for a people, i.e., an aggregate of human beings, or for an aggregate of peoples. Since these individuals or peoples must influence one another, they need to live in a state of right under a unifying will: that is, they require a *constitution* in order to enjoy their rights. A condition in which the individual members of a people are related to each other in this way is said to be a *civil* one, and when considered as a whole in relation to its own members, it is called a *state*. Since the state takes the form of a union created by common interests of everyone living in a state of right, it is called a *commonwealth*.[8]

Politics, for Kant, is thus an act that endows order upon a "multitude of rational beings."[9]

---

6. Rousseau, *The Social Contract*, 54.
7. Immanuel Kant, "The Metaphysics of Morals." In *Kant: Political Writings*, edited by Hans Reiss (Cambridge: Cambridge University Press, 1991), 138.
8. Ibid., 136–37.
9. Kant, quoted in Hannah Arendt, *Lectures on Kant's Political Philosophy* (Chicago: University of Chicago Press, 1992), 17.

To conclude this brief genealogy of politics as a form of ordering, we might mention one of the last representatives of this school of thought: John Rawls.[10] Examining Rawls from this perspective allows us to underscore the extent to which the antagonism between neoliberalism and the "social-liberal" tradition, developed by Rawls or Amartya Sen, is both less radical and less interesting than it may at first appear. For both Rawls and Sen, the central problem of politics is reconciling liberal principles with the need for social cohesion and the preservation of the political community's authority. In other words, Rawls' and Sen's position might be best described as "national-liberalism," which is based on the idea that it is necessary to halt the application of liberal values at the moment at which they risk injuring the imperative of national unity. For the neoliberals, on the contrary, it is precisely when these values challenge concepts such as society, unity, or the political (or national) community, and question the very foundation upon which these concepts are based, that they become interesting.

In *A Theory of Justice*, Rawls' manner of posing the problem of the political community is analogous to that of Rousseau and Kant. Admittedly, Rawls affirms pluralism as the essential point of departure for a liberal analysis, but it is precisely the point of departure for his analysis, not its end point. In other words, Rawls' entire theory of justice-as-equality is about the search for an apparatus that might unify and order society despite an initial condition of pluralism—what Rawls calls a "basic structure" or a "minimum consensus."[11] Thus, once again, the problem of social and political order is about assembling deeply divided individuals and arriving at some kind of consensus despite a diversity of interests and beliefs: "political liberalism tries to answer the question: how is it possible that there can be a stable and just society whose free and equal citizens

---

10. We might equally mention, of course, Jürgen Habermas, whose *Between Facts and Norms: Contributions to a Discourse Theory of Law and Democracy* (Cambridge: MIT Press, 1998) proffers the law as a mechanism of integration and cohesion, the means of constructing procedural "reciprocity" in a highly differentiated world.

11. See John Rawls, *A Theory of Justice* (Cambridge: Harvard University Press, 1999), 7–11.

are deeply divided?"[12] Rawls continues speaking a language of order and unity characteristic of this mode of analysis and episteme. Indeed, he wants to discover

> how a well-ordered democratic society of justice as fairness may establish and preserve unity and stability given the reasonable pluralism characteristic of it. In such a society, a reasonable comprehensive doctrine cannot secure the basis of social unity, nor can it provide the content of public reason on fundamental political questions. Thus, to see how a well-ordered society can be unified and stable, we introduce another basic idea of political liberalism to go with the idea of a political conception of justice, namely the idea of an overlapping consensus of reasonable comprehensive doctrines.[13]

---

12.   John Rawls, *Political Liberalism* (New York: Columbia University Press, 2005), 133.

13.   Ibid., 133–34. It is striking that even an author like Will Kymlicka, who calls for a new conception of citizenship for our multicultural age, one that would open the way for the establishment of special minority rights, nonetheless continues to insist that these new rights will not threaten "national unity." Because his project is inscribed within the liberal paradigm of contract and law, Kymlicka is condemned to pursue his work as a reflection on the "ties that bind," the "authority of the political community," and the feeling of belonging to a "common culture" (in his words). And for him, the redefinition of citizenship he proposes is precisely that which will fulfill this new "inclusive" function. See Will Kymlicka, *Multicultural Citizenship: A Liberal Theory of Minority Rights* (Oxford: Clarendon Press, 1996).

6

UNDOING SOCIETY

Of course, one could object to this genealogy on the grounds that the analyses provided by Rousseau, Kant, Rawls, or Habermas are all very different from each other, and that their conceptions of the law, the state, sovereignty, and community are not interchangeable. Speaking of these theorists as if they belong to a single school of thought thus amounts to a violent simplification and decontextualization of their respective works.

But for the theorists of neoliberalism, such distinctions of content are of little importance. For them, the essence of this tradition lies elsewhere. It exists on a different and higher plane and relates to what we might call their perceptual framework, or the way they conceptualize politics and problematize the very notion of society. What the neoliberals call into question, which begins with Rousseau and Kant, is more like a disposition or a shared manner of posing questions. In their view, Enlightenment philosophy is, above all, characterized by a preoccupation with plurality and diversity. Multiplicity and individuality are conceived as phenomena that make it necessary to invent mechanisms, apparatuses, or institutions for producing unity and coherence—the common. The constitution of a "people," sovereignty, or a body politic is systematically articulated as necessitating the suppression of the "particular" through the creation of a "universal" framework to which subjects must submit.

The social contract theorists have inscribed an obsession for unity and order within contemporary thought. The desire to continuously impose "cohesion" onto the world is one of the essential impulses of modern social and political theory. It can be found across a range of otherwise very different ideological discourses. Evidence of the influence exercised by this mode of thinking can be seen in the fact that even discourses that frame themselves as opposed to the Enlightenment nevertheless recognize the relevance of this mode of thought and sometimes even appropriate its ideas and premises. The socialist and sociological traditions of Saint-Simon and Durkheim are prime examples of this. These authors obviously have very little in common with Rousseau or Kant. Yet, whereas they do not approach questions of the subject, the law, or politics in the same way, their conception of society is nonetheless based on a similarly unifying vision, one that proceeds as the search for integration, cohesion, and the production of consensus: the collective must assert its regulatory power over such agents of societal ferment as individualism, minority movements, and competition between particular interests.[1] Indeed the texts in which Durkheim discusses Hobbes or Rousseau are particularly instructive on this point. It is striking that the author of *Suicide*[2] accepts and appropriates the same problematic and analytical framework proffered by these philosophers: namely, how to conceive of solidarity, of common and impersonal goals, in the face of egoistic and anti-social passions? Only their proposed solution differs: for the sociologist, society as community does not issue from an artificial political act, but is a *sui generis* natural reality resulting from human interaction and association.[3]

It is precisely this mode of analysis the neoliberals call into question: their fundamental objective is to interrogate this obsession with constructing something on the order of "the community." The

---

1. On the affinities between the social contract theorists and Durkheim, see Didier Eribon, *D'une révolution conservatrice et de ses effets sur la gauche française* (Paris: Léo Scheer, 2007).
2. Émile Durkheim, *Suicide: A Study in Sociology*, translated by John A. Spaulding and George Simpson (London: Routledge, 2002).
3. See, for example, Émile Durkheim, *Hobbes à l'agrégation* (Paris: Éditions de l'EHESS, 2011); and *Le Contrat social de Rousseau* (Paris: Kimé, 2008).

idea that theorizing society or politics requires one imagine the establishment of a supra-individual entity—which in turn implies the necessity of creating a transcendent framework in relation to plurality and the play of particular interests—is totally foreign to their thought. It even strikes them as dangerous. In a sense, it is no exaggeration to say the neoliberal theoreticians attempt to deconstruct, or even destroy, the very notion of "society," understood as a phenomenon that assembles people over and above their individual differences. (Of course, it must be emphasized here that the whole issue is to show the extent to which notions like the "common" or the "general" are in fact hollow concepts. It is not a matter of privileging the "individual" over the "general," or the "local" over the "global." The aim of the neoliberals is not to reverse these values, but to refute the entire oppositional system as such. They question its relevance and the extent to which it is actually representative of reality. Their goal is to deconstruct this entire conceptual framework in order to highlight the extremely problematic nature of the vision it propagates and the dangers it entails, particularly from a political point of view).

A good example of this critique can be found in the texts Isaiah Berlin dedicated to what he called the "Counter-Enlightenment"; that is, texts produced by a collection of authors who defined themselves against the theoreticians of the Enlightenment and their heirs. Berlin's account is all about revealing the Enlightenment's obsession with the fantasy of a "harmonious totality," and the desire to establish a society of rational beings who pursue collective or communitarian ends under a cloak of unanimity. The fundamental presupposition of this line of thought, for Berlin, is "men are permanently so constituted (this is offered as an axiom, both psychological and sociological) as to seek after peace, not war, harmony, not discord, unity, not multiplicity":

> Strife, conflict, competition between human beings are essentially pathological processes: men may be so built that these tendencies are, at a certain stage of their development, inevitable; what makes them abnormal is that they do not fulfill those ends that

men as men cannot avoid having in common—the common and permanent purposes that make men human.[4]

According to Berlin, the shared gesture made by those authors categorized under the term "Counter-Enlightenment"—and who have, for this reason, largely been perceived and labeled as conservative or reactionary—was to reject the Enlightenment view, reject the obsession with unity, and reject the constant desire to endow society with coherence. For the neoliberals, the plurality of the social and cultural world is irreducible. It is not merely the foil against which some political theory or other defines itself, but must constitute an end in itself. The "common world," the "collective," the "general will," and the perpetual search for something on the order of the "universal," are myths, and dangerous myths at that.

Berlin specifically cites the work of Johann Gottfried von Herder and Edmund Burke. Both of these thinkers defined themselves against the typical "monism" of the Enlightenment. In their view, this vision necessarily presupposes the possibility of finding a singular, final, and universal solution to humanity's problems. For Counter-Enlightenment thinkers, however, "there are many ideals worth pursuing, [and] some of them are incompatible with [others]."[5] In this sense, the idea of an "all-embracing solution to all human problems which, if there is too much resistance to it, might need force to secure it, only tends to lead to bloodshed and the increase of human misery."[6]

This same affirmation is found in the work of Herder, who argues there is never one and only one valid answer to the great questions confronting humanity: "different civilizations pursue different goals and they are entitled to pursue them."[7] Consequently, political theory must take notice of this diversity rather than try to reduce it through unifying systems: "Herder thought different envi-

4. Isaiah Berlin, *The Sense of Reality* (New York: Farrar, Straus and Giroux, 1996), 120.
5. Berlin, *Conversations with Isaiah Berlin*, 47.
6. Ibid.
7. Ibid., 69.

ronments, different origins, different languages, different tastes and different aspirations. If you allowed that there can be more than one valid answer to a problem, that in itself is a great discovery. It leads to liberalism and toleration."[8] And in the work of Burke, the same pluralistic intent compelled him to question the idea of a "universal human nature." There is no "natural man" or "rational man" who is everywhere the same. People are always already different in their arts, their culture, their habits, their tastes, their character, etc.[9]

Gesturing beyond the particular polemic between the Enlightenment and Counter-Enlightenment theorists, however, Berlin attempts to highlight the fact that Western intellectual, political, and ideological space is characterized by a fundamental confrontation between two temperaments, two attitudes, and two irreducible ways of problematizing the concept of society and understanding the nature of human interaction:

> The history of political thought has, to a large degree, consisted in a duel between . . . two great rival conceptions of society. On the one side stands the advocates of pluralism and variety and an open market for ideas, an order of things that involves clashes and constant need for conciliation, adjustment, balance, an order that is always in a condition of imperfect equilibrium. . . . On the other side are to be found those who believe that this precarious condition is a form of chronic social and personal disease, since health consists in unity, peace, the elimination of the very possibility of disagreement, the recognition of only one end or set of non-conflicting ends as being alone rational, with the corollary that rational disagreement can affect only means.[10]

The representatives of this second tradition are Plato, Spinoza, Helvétius, Rousseau, Fichte, and Hegel. And for Berlin, Marx was also a member of this tradition. Contrary to appearances, then, communism is not a theory of conflict and plurality: it is one of the last incarnations of political monism. For Marx, argues Berlin, "the

---

8.   Ibid., 73.
9.   Ibid., 68.
10.   Berlin, *The Sense of Reality*, 121.

contradictions and conflicts inherent in social development are mere variations on the theme of the uninterrupted progress of humans conceived as a system of beings engaged in understanding and controlling their environment and themselves."[11]

---

11. Ibid., 121–22.

7

LIBERAL AND CONSERVATIVE ETHICS

The author upon whom Foucault most relies when reflecting on the relationship between society, totalization, and multiplicity is Friedrich Hayek. The Austrian economist was one of the principal architects of the neoliberal deconstruction of political philosophy's traditional concepts, such as a "common world," the "public good," or the "general will." For Hayek, discourses employing these concepts are always necessarily shot through with pretensions for order and control, by a desire to control individual behavior, and by the intention to limit life's diversity on behalf of ostensibly "superior" values.

Hayek in fact devoted a well-known article to the uses of the term "social." It is common in political or ideological discourse, argued Hayek, to honor and valorize "social" behavior: conduct aligning with general as opposed to particular interests that contributes to the good of the "people," the "nation," or "society." For Hayek, however, we must be wary of such injunctions: they presuppose, implicitly or explicitly, "the existence of known and common aims"[1] and thereby proffer a view of society as a "whole." More seriously, this representation necessarily nurtures a profoundly au-

---

1. Friedrich Hayek, "What is 'Social'—What Does it Mean?" In *Studies in Philosophy, Politics and Economics* (London: Routledge, 1967), 242.

thoritarian "desire" to see "all individual activity directed towards defined 'social' aims and tasks subordinated to the interests of the 'community.'"[2] Doctrines such as these are anything but neutral. They do not merely valorize the universal over the local, but work in tandem with mechanisms of political domination and social control by giving "precedence to certain [particular] values."[3] For what is referred to as the "interests of society" are really, most of the time, the interests "of the majority."[4]

Just as Berlin contrasted two great rival conceptions of society, Hayek distinguished between two great rival political ethics. And, strikingly, Hayek distinguishes these ethics on the basis of their relation to order and disorder. On the one hand, Hayek posits a conservative attitude that, of course, characterizes "conservatives" in the traditional sense of this term, but Hayek argues it equally characterizes the socialists. Hayek offers an interesting observation in this regard: in the history of ideas, it is extremely common to see socialists become conservative and convert to conservatism over a number of years. It is much more rare for socialists to become liberals. That it is more common for the "repentant socialist to find a new spiritual home in the conservative fold than in the liberal"[5] is not, for Hayek, a matter of chance. It is rather symptomatic of a profound affinity between conservatism and socialism, while liberalism obeys an entirely different value system.

What most fundamentally unites the conservative and the socialist is an affinity for order, tendencies toward paternalism, and the adoration of power. This attitude is manifest most notably in their shared anxiety about novelty, social change, and the unprecedented:

> One of the fundamental traits of the conservative attitude is a fear of change, a timid distrust of the new as such, while the liberal position is based on courage and confidence, on a prepar-

---

2. Ibid., 240.
3. Ibid., 243.
4. Ibid., 242.
5. Hayek, "Why I am Not a Conservative," 402.

edness to let change run its course even if we cannot predict where it will lead.[6]

One of the essential characteristics of conservativism is, consequently, a predilection for authority. But this is a predilection that takes different forms in different traditions: the conservative praises the nation and nationalism, the Enlightenment philosopher calls for the subordination of particularism to the *volonté générale*, the socialist claims to restore a sense of "collectivity" or "commonality" to a world governed by individualism, etc. But what we find manifest in each tradition is the same disdain for spontaneity, or anything that escapes regulatory power—in short, we find the same drive to control plurality by establishing a transcendent imperative: "the conservative feels safe and content only if he is assured that some higher wisdom watches and supervises change, only if he knows that some authority is charged with keeping the change 'orderly.'"[7]

The neoliberal ethic arises in opposition to this inclination for order. It seeks to rid political theory and philosophy of the authoritarian impulses rooted in their unifying and monistic conceptions of the social order. Neoliberalism thus situates itself on the side of disorder, immanence, and, therefore, pluralism. A neoliberal world can never be unified or totalized. It is not built upon the horizon of a commons-to-come; it is conceived as essentially plural, and therefore animated by contradictory and irreconcilable logics:

> When I say that the conservative lacks principles, I do not mean to suggest that he lacks moral conviction. The typical conservative is indeed usually a man of very strong moral convictions. What I mean is that he has no political principles which enable him to work with people whose moral values differ from his own for a political order in which both can obey their convictions. It is the recognition of such principles that permits the coexistence of different sets of values that makes it possible to build a peaceful society with a minimum of force. The acceptance of such

---

6. Ibid., 400.
7. Ibid.

principles means that we agree to tolerate much that we dislike.
There are many values of the conservative which appeal to me
more than those of the socialists; yet for a liberal the importance
he personally attaches to specific goals is not sufficient justification for forcing others to serve them.[8]

Neoliberal social theory thus seeks to refute the idea that we need a
superior "plan" to bring about "consensus" between individuals, or
the necessity of a "contract" suppressing particular interests on behalf of more general demands. We should, instead, imagine a fundamentally plural world that does not repress diverse modes of life,
but which rather permits social contradictions to express themselves. It is precisely in this context that the neoliberal speaks of a
"market utopia": the market is conceived as a means to enable a
"spontaneous order based on abstract rules that leaves individuals
free to use their own knowledge for their own purposes."[9] The
market is not a form of organization. It is not based on the idea of
harmony, unity, or coherence, but is rather open to heterogeneity:

> In contrast to an organization, neither has a spontaneous social
> order a purpose nor need there be agreement on the concrete
> results it will produce in order to agree on the desirability of
> such an order, because, being independent of any particular pur-
> pose, *it can be used for, and will assist in the pursuit of, a great
> many different, divergent and even conflicting individual pur-
> poses. Thus the order of the market, in particular, rests not on
> common purposes.*[10]

This property of the market, for Hayek, allows contradictory realities to emerge in spontaneous, uncontrollable, and unpredictable
ways. This explains the resistance the market incites:

8.   Ibid., 401–2.
9.   Friedrich Hayek, "The Principles of a Liberal Social Order." In *Studies in Philosophy, Politics and Economics* (London: Routledge, 1967), 162.
10.   Ibid., 163, emphasis added.

There is perhaps no single factor contributing so much to people's frequent reluctance to let the market work as their inability to conceive how some necessary balance, between demand and supply, between exports and imports, or the like, will be brought about without deliberate control.[11]

---

11.   Hayek, "Why I am Not a Conservative," 400.

8

IMMANENCE, HETEROGENEITY, AND MULTIPLICITY

The essential project of every neoliberal thinker is to deconstruct totalizing visions of the social world. To put it differently, their singular contribution to intellectual history has been their ability to undermine one of the implicit foundations of traditional social theory and political philosophy: namely, the idea that plurality and heterogeneity are negative poles against which it becomes necessary to erect such concepts as "sovereignty," "society," "the political," etc. The market form opens up the possibility of theorizing the world without invoking a transcendent framework (whether in political, legal, or sociological form) designed to unify and organize social plurality. Neoliberalism proffers an image of the world as essentially disorganized: it is a world without a center, without unity, without consistency, without meaning.[1] Neoliberal thought thus checks what Didier Eribon calls "Hegelian or synthetic conceptions" of reality—that is, interpretive frameworks that are unable to

---

1. In a certain sense, neoliberal theory applies the logic of a free market of ideas, conceptualized as a purely formal matrix that is open to disputation, to the social world. See Marcela Iacub, *De la pornographie en Amérique* (Paris: Fayard, 2010), 102.

think in terms of plurality or heterogeneity because they always seek to achieve "convergence" or "alliance."[2]

In many ways, it was precisely this attempt to disqualify unifying analytical frameworks that captivated Michel Foucault. He never ceases to insist, in *The Birth of Biopolitics*, on the way in which neoliberal theory nullifies the possibility of a "would-be central, totalizing bird's-eye view."[3] As Foucault puts it:

> *Homo economicus* is the one island of rationality possible within an economic process whose uncontrollable nature does not challenge, but instead founds the rationality of the atomistic behavior of *homo economicus*. Thus the economic world is naturally opaque and naturally non-totalizable. It is originally and definitively constituted from a multiplicity of points of view which is all the more irreducible as this same multiplicity assures their ultimate and spontaneous convergence. *Economics is an atheistic discipline; economics is a discipline without a God; economics is a discipline without totality*; economics is a discipline that begins to demonstrate not only the pointlessness, but also the impossibility of a sovereign point of view over the totality of the state that he has to govern.[4]

And as he further concludes,

> Liberalism acquired its modern shape precisely with the formulation of this essential incompatibility between the non-totalizable multiplicity of economic subjects of interest and the totalizing unity of the juridical sovereign.[5]

The somewhat exaggerated fashion in which Foucault takes up the neoliberal theme of "multiplicity" and shows how it produces a conception of society freed from all transcendence (economics as an

---

2. Didier Eribon, "Réponses et principes," *French Cultural Studies*, 2012. Also see "Les frontières et le temps de la politique," Concluding Panel at the Sexual Nationalisms Conference, Amsterdam, January 26–28, 2011.
3. Foucault, *The Birth of Biopolitics*, 292.
4. Ibid., 282.
5. Ibid.

atheistic discipline, without God, without totality, etc.) should not, however, be interpreted as tacit assent of the neoliberal paradigm by the author of *Discipline and Punish*. Rather, what interests Foucault is the powerful idea that there is a desire to control implicit in every totalizing discourse. Unifying theories are necessarily structured by impulses for order. Because they call for the constitution of a transcendent perspective, they reproduce the effects of power and domination by virtue of their very form. In short, they are forms of thought complicit with sovereignty.

If this critique is especially important to Foucault, it is because it corresponds to one of the principle critiques of Marxism (as well as psychoanalysis) he had been voicing since the mid-1970s. His discussion of neoliberalism should therefore be situated in the context of Foucault's reflections on the problem of resistance and his interrogation of the conditions for producing a radical critique of the social order: what type of theory is best able to produce emancipatory effects? What analytic offers the best possibility of understanding mechanisms of power, and is thus best able to destabilize or counteract them?

Marxism, according to Foucault's critique, is an insufficient doctrine because it is insufficiently critical. At first glance, Marxism appears to be a theory that challenges the very foundations of the social and economic order by offering instruments for destabilizing, abolishing, and even moving beyond this order. But the essential problem with Marxism, in Foucault's view, is its failure to interrogate the totalizing character of its own discourse: it fully embraces the ambition to construct a unified vision of society—which is to say the ambition to shape what happens in society according to a certain number of elementary and predetermined principles. At the very moment in which Marxism claims to furnish weapons against domination, it actually reproduces effects of power, authority, and censorship. Adopting this totalizing perspective means, on the one hand, Marxism is not only unable to challenge the idea of sovereignty, but it even represents one of the possible modalities through which sovereignty is exercised. And by organizing its conception of society according to its own "transcendental" framework, Marxism also necessarily disables particular struggles, as well as both present and future marginal realities, from escaping its all-encompassing hermeneutic grid.

In his 1976 lecture series at the Collège de France, titled *Society Must be Defended*,[6] Foucault formulates this critique of Marxism alongside other "totalizing" theories (which also includes psychoanalysis, perhaps the dominant international manifestation of contemporary totalizing thought). According to Foucault, one of the most important developments since the 1960s—and 1968 in particular—was the appearance of a multitude of "dispersed," "discontinuous," "particular," and "local" movements struggling against psychiatric institutions, traditional moral or sexual hierarchies, judicial and penal apparatuses, etc.[7] What strikes Foucault is the extreme productivity of these local discourses. He evokes the "astonishing efficacy of discontinuous, particular, and local critiques."[8] The proliferation of particular struggles, in Foucault's view, helped give voice to "a sort of general feeling that the ground was crumbling beneath our feet, especially in places where it seemed most familiar, most solid, and closest to us, to our bodies, to our everyday gestures."[9]

Of course, the author of *Discipline and Punish* does not stop at this observation but moves on to insist these local struggles were only possible in the context of a larger criticism of totalizing theories: these minority struggles only emerged through a more general struggle against centralizing paradigms. They consisted of "subjugated knowledges," or "historical contents that have been buried or masked in functional coherences or formal systemizations."[10] "Subjugated knowledges," writes Foucault, "are, then, blocks of historical knowledges that were present in the functional and systematic ensembles, but which were masked, and [these] critiques [were]

---

6. Michel Foucault, *Society Must be Defended: Lectures at the Collège de France, 1975-1976*, translated by David Macey (New York: Picador, 2003).
7. Ibid., 5–6.
8. Ibid., 6.
9. Ibid.
10. Ibid., 7.

able to reveal their existence."[11] Foucault considers the knowledges of the "psychiatrized," the "patient," the "nurse," the "delinquent"—in short, the knowledges of people forgotten by Marxism but which one would not describe as "common knowledge or common sense but, on the contrary, a particular knowledge, a knowledge that is local, regional, or differential, incapable of unanimity."[12] What is at issue here for Foucault, in other words, is the capacity to play these "local, discontinuous, disqualified, or nonlegitimized knowledges off against the unitary theoretical instance that claims to be able to filter them [and] organize them into a hierarchy."[13]

In these lectures, Foucault thus opposes two modes of critique: there is, on the one hand, those discourses that operate according to the notion of "totality" and, on the other hand, there are these dispersed, non-centralized critiques that "do not need a visa from some common regime to establish [their] validity."[14] For Foucault, genealogies and archaeologies of power cannot be carried out and unfolded to their greatest extent without "the removal of the tyranny of totalizing discourses":[15] "totalitarian theories" (in Foucault's phrase) like Marxism or psychoanalysis produce a fundamentally "inhibiting effect"; they exude "the effect of putting the brakes on."[16] They may, at times, furnish locally useful instruments, but only on the condition that "the theoretical unity of their discourse is, so to speak, suspended, or at least cut up, ripped up, torn to shreds, turned inside out, displaced, caricatured, dramatized, theatricalized, and so on."[17]

At base, the essential argument Foucault defends is the idea that totalizing discourses necessarily produce, often despite themselves, subjugating and hierarchical effects. They "marginalize" the experience of certain subjects. But genealogy is always situated on the

11. Ibid.
12. Ibid., 7–8.
13. Ibid., 9.
14. Ibid., 6.
15. Ibid., 8.
16. Ibid., 6.
17. Ibid.

other side of this process. It tries to reveal the underside of totalizing discourses. It is defined as a project seeking to "desubjugate historical knowledges, to set them free, or in other words, to enable them to oppose and struggle against the coercion of a unitary, formal, and scientific theoretical discourse."[18]

The development of critical thinking thus requires the capacity to be attentive to the diverse struggles that arise within social space, and to follow their emergence in order to grasp their singularity. One must adopt an attitude of openness to the unprecedented—and, consequently, renounce the hermeneutical grids fixing perception and predetermining the ways in which we see the world. For these grids produce forms of domination and concealment; they participate in power's exercise more than they reveal power's mechanisms. A critical theory must free itself from the temptation to totalize. It must renounce paradigms that attempt to endow "general" coherence onto that which occurs at the local level.

As discussed previously, the neoliberal deconstruction of "monistic" and unifying paradigms led to a valorization of notions such as immanence, plurality, and multiplicity (the market form represents a mechanism that opens the possibility of imagining an incoherent and heterogeneous society, above which no unifying horizon can arise). "Immanence," "plurality," and "multiplicity": these are concepts Foucault situates at the heart of his theory of power.

Foucault developed this approach in the section of *A History of Sexuality* dedicated to the elaboration of a "Method" (his term) of analyzing power. Why does this discussion on method seem necessary to him? Because the word "power," which he uses throughout his work, "is apt to lead to a number of misunderstandings—misunderstandings with respect to its nature, its form, and its unity."[19] Foucault is speaking specifically of theories that tend to produce an overly unifying and centralized conception of power; theories that speak of "power" in terms of "a group of institutions and mecha-

---

18.   Ibid., 10.
19.   Michel Foucault, *The History of Sexuality, Volume 1: An Introduction*, translated by Robert Hurley (New York: Vintage Books, 1979), 92.

nisms that ensure the subservience of the citizens of a given state"
(such as the social contract theorists) or those for whom power
designates "a general system of domination exerted by one group
over another, a system whose effects, through successive deriva-
tions, pervade the entire social body" (such as in sociological or
Marxist theories).[20] Against these transcendental paradigms that
think in terms of unity and totality, Foucault proposes a different
conception of power informed by notions of immanence and multiplicity: "it seems to me that power must be understood in the first
instance as the multiplicity of force relations immanent in the sphere
in which they operate and which constitute their own organization."[21]

Rendering the exercise of power intelligible in its most "periph-
eral effects" demands a point of view that does not assign "power" a
place or origin, and does not presuppose the existence of "a central
point" or a "unique source" from which the mechanisms of control
spread: "power's condition of possibility . . . is the moving substrate
of force relations which, by virtue of their inequality, constantly
engenders states of power, but the latter are always local and un-
stable."[22] What emerges, consequently, is an "omnipresence of
power":

> Not because it has the privilege of consolidating everything
> under its invincible unity, but because it is produced from one
> moment to the next, at every point, or rather in every relation
> from one point to another. Power is everywhere; not because it
> embraces everything, but because it comes from everywhere.[23]

20. Ibid., 92.
21. Ibid.
22. Ibid., 93.
23. Ibid.

9

SKEPTICISM AND THE POLITICS OF SINGULARITIES

"There is no such thing as society." This statement, typical of neoliberal doctrine, is often perceived to be an extremely strong ideological marker. It is a slogan rallying all those who claim an individualist philosophy, as well as those who wage a political war against socially inspired reforms and a theory-based war against sociology in particular. But, in a sense, this idea perfectly expresses the type of critique Foucault tried to develop during the 1970s: power is exercised in a diffuse manner; it is everywhere, and it functions in a disseminated fashion. The partial, local, and differential struggles that arise on a regular basis are not inscribed within a larger and more global framework. It is not necessary to place them within such a framework in order to understand them and grasp their meaning.

These struggles carry their own value and their own significance within themselves. According to a view that approximates Nietzsche's conception of the event (Being is an aggregate of a plurality of events), Foucault contends there is nothing called "society" in which struggles and mobilizations arise from time to time; rather these struggles and mobilizations should be theorized on their own terms, independent of any larger horizon. For Foucault, totalizing theories erase the plurality, heterogeneity, and incoherence of the social world; they repress local struggles and prevent them from attaining visibility. (In other words, the expression "there is no such thing as society," reinterpreted in this sense, does not deny the existence of the social, but rather denies the process of totalization taking place when we imagine an object like "society." It is this unification that doesn't exist and whose reality is contested, not the idea of the social world as such.)

The construction of this new analytic of power led Foucault, as we know, to create a new image of the intellectual. If struggles unfold in a local or regional context, if they escape totalizing frameworks, then the intellectual must become a "'specific' intellectual."[1] The intellectual must renounce the figure—imposed by Sartre in particular, but also prominent in Marxism—of the universal intellectual, which is to say the intellectual who "listens as the representative of the universal," as the "conscious/conscience of everyone."[2] The universal intellectual approaches particular struggles with large concepts and pre-fabricated discourses. Consequently, the universal intellectual integrates local struggles into the framework of a more general struggle carried out on behalf of values like justice, the ideal law, communism-to-come, etc. Conversely, the specific intellectual refuses this constant temptation to resignify, recode, or recolonize local struggles within a universal discourse. Foucault thus calls for the invention of a new relationship between theory and practice, which, according to him, had already begun to develop since the end of the 1960s:

> Intellectuals have become accustomed to working not in the character of the "universal," the "exemplary," the "just-and-true for all," but in specific sectors, at precise points where they are situated either by their professional conditions of work or their conditions of life (housing, the hospital, the asylum, the laboratory, the university, familial and sexual relations). Through this they have undoubtedly gained a much more concrete awareness

---

1. Michel Foucault, "The Political Function of the Intellectual." *Radical Philosophy*, vol. 17 (Summer, 1977), 12.
2. Ibid.

of struggles. They have also thereby encountered problems which are specific, "non-universal," often different from those of the proletariat and the masses.[3]

It seems particularly important to address this point further, because it is striking to observe how we find an almost identical gesture among the neoliberals. For them too, criticism of the role of universals and the transcendental in social and political theory likewise led to the critique of the figure of the universal intellectual, or better, the critique of the idea that the intellectual is capable of forming a synthetic vision of society.

Indeed, the neoliberals constantly opposed the attitude that accords thought with disproportionate power. This attitude is characteristic of Marxism, but it was in fact born with the Enlightenment, particularly in Voltaire and Rousseau. The philosophers of the Enlightenment fabricated a philosophical myth that portended dangerous political consequences: the omnipotence of the intellect. They believed reason possessed unlimited power, and they acted as if it was possible to ordain society's form and to build society according to a plan forged in the mind. The Enlightenment philosophers thus proceeded according to a "constructivist rationalism." They thought "independently existing reason [was] capable of designing civilization (see the statement by Voltaire: 'If you want good laws, burn those you have and make new ones')."[4] The rationalism of the Enlightenment refused to recognize the limits of reason. Indeed, it legitimized a form of intellectual narcissism that encouraged scholars and philosophers to think the world revolved around them, insofar as they were the only ones capable of escaping partiality and attaining a total view of society. This "false intellectualism" often led to a belief in the merits of government by scholars and experts.

The neoliberal ethic rejects this conception of thought and offers a more modest doctrine. It adopts a humble posture that recognizes and accepts its own boundaries and limitations. Far from thinking

---

3.   Ibid.
4.   Friedrich Hayek, "The Principles of a Liberal Social Order." In *Studies in Philosophy, Politics and Economics* (London: Routledge, 1967), 160.

the social order can be deduced from an *a priori* theoretical construct, the neoliberal ethic believes the social order is made up of multiple and spontaneous forces that, as a matter of principle, escape human knowledge and any vision claiming totality:

> Personally I believe that this false rationalism, which gained influence in the French Revolution and which during the past hundred years has exercised its influence mainly through the twin movements of Positivism and Hegelianism, is an expression of an intellectual hubris which is the opposite of that intellectual humility which is the essence of true liberalism that regards with reverence those spontaneous social forces through which the individual creates things greater than he knows.[5]

One can thus understand the sense in which neoliberal philosophy is rooted in a philosophy of knowledge whose point of departure is the acceptance of the limits of thought. The scholars cannot see everything and cannot know everything. They must renounce as folly the ambition to understand and master the plethora of diverse processes developing within the world. As a matter of principle, much escapes them:

> Liberalism thus derives from the discovery of a self-generating or spontaneous order in social affairs (the same discovery which led to the recognition that there existed an object for theoretical social sciences), an order which made it possible to utilize the knowledge and skill of all members of society to a much greater extent than would be possible in any order created by central direction, and the consequent desire to make as full use of these powerful spontaneous ordering forces as possible.[6]

Neoliberal theory is thus a skeptical doctrine. It proceeds from the principle of the narrow limits of human understanding—which is

---

5. Friedrich Hayek, "Opening Address to a Conference at Mont Pèlerin." In *Studies in Philosophy, Politics and Economics* (London: Routledge, 1967), 155.
6. Hayek, "The Principles of a Liberal Social Order," 162.

why David Hume is one of neoliberalism's most important theoretical references.[7]

Foucault would undoubtedly not subscribe to all of these propositions. He does not formulate his analysis in the same terms, nor does he use the same words. But in many ways, Foucault found a similar preoccupation in neoliberalism in terms of adopting an attitude that allows one to remain attentive, open, and receptive to the multiplicity of emergent facts within the social world. Theories with universal pretensions and grand narratives mask and distort reality at the very moment they claim to grasp it. By predetermining our frameworks and analytical categories, these theories above all prevent us from perceiving what is being invented: they prevent us from seeing novelty when it is produced, and thus prevent us from grasping its singularity.

This is why it would not be incorrect to portray Foucault, as Paul Veyne has proposed,[8] in the guise of skeptical thinker, a philosopher who rejects the value of universals, transcendentals, generalized ideas, as someone committed to moving beyond any reference to Truth, Morality, Value, etc. Nevertheless, I cannot accept the argument, proffered by this historian of antiquity, that invokes Foucault's radical skepticism in order to deny the political nature of his work and life. According to Veyne, the Foucauldian critique of universals and abstract ideas removes any possibility of endowing political action with a foundation or justification. Political action is therefore always arbitrary and, in a sense, absurd. Foucault accordingly maintained a position of profound doubt and distance from politics—an approach that is very far from the "myth" of the leftist activist philosopher that predominates in France and the United States.

In my opinion, Foucault's skepticism should not be viewed as a form of disengagement, or an attitude that leads, almost necessarily, to depoliticization. On the contrary, the critique of "general" ideas,

---

7. See Friedrich Hayek, "The Legal and Political Philosophy of David Hume." In *Studies in Philosophy, Politics and Economics* (London: Routledge, 1967), 106–21.
8. Paul Veyne, *Foucault: His Thought, His Character* (London: Polity, 2010).

"totalizing" theories, or "fundamentalist" thinking constitutes the starting point for the invention of a new politics, which we could define as the politics of singularities, a politics accompanying and supporting multiple local struggles. Foucault's approach is fundamentally about freeing thought from the myths and attitudes forbidding it from becoming simultaneously radical and effective: namely, the obsession with coherence, the universal, collective values, the "meaning of History," etc. All of this prevents us from understanding emergent struggles on their own terms, for what they really are. Foucault's skepticism thus represents the starting point of a project of self-critique designed to purge the habits dogging traditional politics and which are, in reality, depoliticizing, insofar as they render us incapable of understanding the singularity of emergent struggles. In short, Foucault's skepticism is the starting point for the reinvention of an emancipatory politics.

10

TO NOT BE GOVERNED

We are so accustomed to thinking of neoliberalism as a dominant ideology, as a hegemonic system against which we must mobilize, that associating neoliberalism with struggles and practices of resistance and emancipation jars our basic conceptual categories. Nevertheless, it is striking to observe how Foucault's discussion of the neoliberal tradition is primarily based on the theme of criticism, of resistance, of the instruments available to us for challenging forms of domination imposed upon us. Of course, Foucault is not naïve: he is well aware the emergence and establishment of neoliberal governmentality has produced mechanisms of power, control, and hierarchy, and its analysis is therefore necessary in order to curb its excesses. But this take on neoliberalism is hardly original: it constitutes the basic premise of most studies of neoliberalism, and these knee-jerk reactions always lead to the same project: a "negative" critique of the neoliberal paradigm that focuses on its dangers and threats.

Foucault's project breaks with this traditional approach: his analysis is more unsettling and his method more complex. Foucault's aim is to alter our spontaneous perception of neoliberal discourse. Accordingly, one of the central ideas in *The Birth of Biopolitics* is that there is something liberating, emancipatory, and critical going on in neoliberalism. Foucault is careful to state this explicitly in the first lecture of the course. At the end of this first lecture, he asks his audience not to mistake his interrogation of liberalism, neoliberalism, his account of its emergence, and his analysis of the properties of this generalized regulatory regime as of merely historical or documentary interest. His exegesis addresses contemporary problems, problems that "arise for us in our immediate and concrete actuality."[1] They concern the present; they shape the situation in which we find ourselves. "What does it mean when we speak of liberalism," writes Foucault, "when we apply a liberal politics to ourselves, today, and what relationship may there be between this and those questions of right that we call freedoms and liberties?"[2] He then formulates a more important, more audacious line of inquiry by making a connection between economic neoliberalism and certain practices of resistance developing in the name of political liberalism: "what is going on in all of this, in today's debate in which Helmut Schmidt's economic principles bizarrely echo the voice of dissidents in the East, in this problem of liberty, of liberalism?"[3] In what way does Foucault substantiate this connection between liberalism and neoliberalism, on the one hand, and dissident movements, on the other? How is neoliberal discourse potentially emancipatory? Or, more precisely, in what way is it possible to find, in this discourse, instruments or weapons with which to carry out political and democratic struggle?

The critical potential inscribed in neoliberal rationality is rooted in the fact that this tradition asserts itself within a framework that opposes the state; or better, opposes state rationality (*la raison d'État*). Indeed, liberalism and neoliberalism are not, at their core, a disposition that is comprised of a corpus of theoretical or philosophical axioms, or an assortment of basic ideological principles. Rather, if we want to describe what most unifies neoliberal intellectuals beyond their often-considerable differences, we need to evoke a character trait, or a collection of quasi-psychological preoccupa-

---

1. Foucault, *The Birth of Biopolitics*, 22.
2. Ibid.
3. Ibid.

tions. In Foucault's view, this common impulse is a "state phobia."[4] Liberals are fundamentally animated by a fear of the state—the intensity of which is illustrated by Foucault's reference to the remarks of art historian Bernard Berenson: "God knows I fear the destruction of the world by the atomic bomb, but there is at least one thing I fear as much, and that is the invasion of humanity by the state."[5] According to Foucault, neoliberalism is built upon the idea that "one always governs too much," or, at the very least, "one should always suspect that one governs too much."[6] In other words, neoliberalism harbors a radical critique of state governmentality. This doctrine is not at all content with seeking out the best means, or the least costly means, of achieving political objectives. Rather, it questions the very possibility of the state itself. It is a response to the question, "why, after all, is it necessary to govern?"[7]

In this sense, it does not seem wrong to suggest that Foucault perceived neoliberalism as a contemporary incarnation of the critical tradition. During a 1978 lecture entitled "What Is Critique?"[8] given only a few months before *The Birth of Biopolitics*, Foucault effectively defined critique as an attitude or a disposition in which one situates oneself on the side of the governed and against forms of government. Of course, Foucault goes on to say the demand for freedom is not based on a dogmatic refusal of all government, but rather issues from a more modest and more diffuse intent. It testifies to a desire to be governed "*like that*, by that, in the name of those principles, with such and such an objective in mind and by means of such procedures, not like that, not for that, not by them."[9] Foucault defines critique as "the art of not being governed quite so much,"[10] and this is also one of the central aspects of neoliberalism.

---

4. Ibid., 76.
5. Quoted in ibid., 75.
6. Ibid., 319.
7. Ibid.
8. See Michel Foucault, "What is Critique?" In *The Politics of Truth*, edited by Sylvère Lotringer (Los Angeles: Semiotext(e), 2007).
9. Ibid., 44.
10. Ibid., 45.

I I

POLITICS, RIGHT, SOVEREIGNTY

If the anti-statism of the neoliberal tradition interests Foucault, it is because it provides a means of deconstructing those paradigms that, according to Foucault, produce obedience in contemporary societies: political philosophy, the theory of law, and trust in the state.

Whenever we discuss Michel Foucault, we mostly talk about his reconceptualization of power: the way in which power, for Foucault, functions in a diffused, dispersed, and scattered fashion. And contemporary societies, in Foucault's view, must accordingly be understood as disciplinary societies in which multiple normalizing apparatuses invest bodies and shape subjectivities. Nevertheless, it seems to me this perspective tends to overshadow another important dimension of Foucault's work: the veritable war he waged against political philosophy and the philosophy of right.

From the mid-1970s onwards, one of Foucault's central concerns was to challenge or deconstruct what he called the "juridical model of sovereignty."[1] Foucault is not referring here to a well-constituted theory, but rather a mode of analysis, a system of representation, or a way of thinking about power that has been characteristic of the West since the Enlightenment, and perhaps even earlier. It is an apparatus built around a number of clearly identifiable concepts:

---

1. Foucault, *Society Must be Defended*, 265.

contract, law, right, general will, etc. Together, these concepts give rise to a whole set of myths, and even mystifications, that shape our view of reality, our perception of the state, and the way we interpret the meaning of politics.

What is most essential about this conceptual grid is its ability to constitute the state as a locus of freedom or liberation: it construes politics as a framework within which men, once freed from their passions and the interplay of particular interests, are able to construct a legitimate order through reason and non-violent deliberation; a *volonté générale* expressed and embodied in the law (the notion of "deliberative democracy" is the latest instantiation of this theme). In short, this system posits a relation between politics, or law, and emancipation: the figure of the citizen, the aspiration of the universal, and the image of the free individual.[2]

Foucault does not of course ignore the subversive role this system played historically—and sometimes continues to play—in terms of contesting the established order. For this is, after all, the rhetoric of the French Revolution and of Rousseau. But Foucault also thinks the rupture introduced into political theory by Enlightenment philosophy tends to be greatly overstated. According to Foucault, the discourse of rights was not invented by the bourgeoisie to oppose the arbitrary authority of monarchical power; on the contrary, it is a system of representation upon which royal power was already based (and which it used against various feudal systems). In other words, Enlightenment discourse did not introduce the rupture in the history of thought we usually suppose. In fact, the defining act of the bourgeoisie was its ability to turn the juridical discourse of monarchical power against those who invented it: "when the bourgeoisie finally rid itself of monarchical power, it did so precisely by using this juridical discourse—which was nonethe-

2.   See, for example, the connection created between the conquest of freedom and the creation of a relatively autonomous public sphere, Hannah Arendt, *Qu'est-ce que la politique?* (Paris: Seuil, 1995). In the contemporary period, it is probably Jürgen Habermas who has most explicitly defended this view.

less that of the monarchy—which it turned against the monarchy itself."[3]

Yet how are we to reconcile Enlightenment thought with the monarchical system? What is the connection between the theory of right, political philosophy, and the figure of the king and the sovereign?

This is the crux of Foucault's analysis and the deconstruction he pursues. He wants to transform our perception of the philosophy of right and political theory. He wants to expose the extent to which the juridico-political axiomatic at work in Rousseau and Hobbes, and up to the work of Rawls, Habermas, and Kymlicka—and even in some of Derrida's work[4]—is not about freedom or individual emancipation. In fact, one of its fundamental properties is its ability to endow legitimacy upon the state and upon political domination; it produces an image of the "subject of law" as a subject that is always-already obedient, always-already subject to a sovereign whose superiority and transcendence they are forced to recognize. In other words, even if this apparatus played a revolutionary role and at times functioned as an instrument for limiting state power on behalf of popular rights, it nevertheless remains firmly within the framework of state rationality and therefore functions in solidarity with the exercise of juridical rationality.

According to Foucault, the problem of political philosophy is, above all, the problem of the sovereign: "when Rousseau came up with his theory of the State, he tried to show . . . a sovereign, moreover a collective sovereign, a sovereign as a social body or, better, a social body as a sovereign."[5] Juridical theory's obsession has always been to determine how it is possible to constitute a "political unity" defined as the "the existence of an individual or collective sovereign who is the holder of part of the totality of these

---

3. Michel Foucault, "The Meshes of Power." In *Space, Knowledge and Power: Foucault and Geography* (Hampshire: Ashgate Publishing, 2007), 155.

4. See Jacques Derrida, *Du droit à la philosophie* (Paris: Galilée, 1990).

5. Foucault, "The Meshes of Power," 155.

individual rights and at the same time the principle of their limitation."[6]

This juridico-deductive axiomatic is not, therefore, situated on
the side of resistance, disobedience, or dissent. It is not situated on
the side of the governed, but on the side of the state. It speaks the
discourse of the state. It exists to find ways for justifying governmental practice and the state's claim to be what it is.[7] To this end, it
constructs a complete fiction about the origin of the state in order to
show how such a power can be constituted "in accordance with a
certain basic legitimacy that is much more than any law and that
allows laws to function as such."[8] And what Foucault intends to
demonstrate is how the conceptualization of this fundamental legitimacy necessarily presupposes the creation of a certain image of the
subject as an obedient subject: the citizen.

This theory of sovereignty is built upon that central figure of
Western philosophy: the subject of right. The subject of right and
sovereignty are two sides of the same coin. One cannot function
without the other. This subject is not, contrary to what is usually
believed, a being who is aware of his rights and who acts in such a
way as to use these rights against the imperatives of state rationality.
On the contrary, this subject acts as a "subject who has to be subjec-
tified":

> What characterizes the subject of right? Of course, at the outset
> he has natural rights. But he becomes a subject of right in a
> positive system only when he has agreed at least to the principle
> of ceding these rights, of relinquishing them, when he has sub-
> scribed to their limitation and has accepted the principle of their

---

6. Foucault, *The Birth of Biopolitics*, 282.
7. This mode of analysis is consubstantially linked to a certain attitude, a way for the
philosopher to subjectify as legislator and to dream of himself as the universal man.
Political theory claims to be neutral. It prefers to arrive after the conflict is settled and it
situates itself in the center, above the fray. Its goal is to produce a kind of armistice by
imagining how to arrive at a reconciliatory order. Generally speaking, then, this mode of
analysis should encourage us to question the relationship between philosophy and the
state, between the philosophical point of view and the state's point of view. See Jean-
Louis Fabiani, *Les Philosophes de la République* (Paris: Minuit, 1988).
8. Foucault, *Society Must be Defended*, 44, emphasis added.

transfer. That is to say, the subject of right is a subject who accepts negativity, who agrees to a self-renunciation and splits himself, as it were, to be, at one level, the possessor of a number of natural and immediate rights, and, at another level, someone who agrees to the principle of relinquishing them and who is thereby constituted as a different subject of right superimposed on the first. The dialectic or mechanism of the subject of right is characterized by the division of the subject, the existence of a transcendence of the second subject in relation to the first, and a relationship of negativity, renunciation, and limitation between them, and it is in this movement that law and the prohibition emerge.[9]

The system of will and right always shapes us in a negative and limiting manner. Far from emphasizing and enhancing our capacity for resistance, disobedience, and dissent, this system functions as a form of subjugation.

Political philosophy is thus situated on the side of order, on the side of the state. It is not a discourse of freedom, autonomy, or individuality. It is a discourse of obedience; it is based on an act that legitimizes the sovereign—or something that represents the sovereign. In other words, it is not on the side of social struggle and it does not furnish instruments of resistance. It furnishes governments with a discourse granting them the right to govern.

Indeed, the idea according to which the juridico-political axiomatic, the language of the social contract, of the general will, and of "politics" essentially works by countering protest movements and mobilizations by reminding them of the political order—and thereby protecting the sovereign from any radical protest that might endanger the foundations of its domination and the belief in its legitimacy—is the principal issue of Foucault's course at the Collège de France titled "Society Must be Defended."

In this course, Foucault takes the work of Hobbes, not Rousseau, as his principal analytical object, and he poses two important questions. First, he asks why, for what reason, in what context, and

9. Foucault, *The Birth of Biopolitics*, 274–75.

against whom did Hobbes write *Leviathan*? And secondly, he asks how we might explain the fact that this book is understood as the founding text of modern political philosophy.

In his reading of Hobbes, Foucault broke with the exegetical method of interpreting philosophical texts in order to show the extent to which *Leviathan* is a political book inscribed within a larger ideological conflict: we cannot understand anything about Hobbes' book if we fail to grasp that Hobbes wrote *Leviathan* with a specific opponent in mind. Specifically, Hobbes opposed a collection of historical discourses circulating and even proliferating in England during the middle of the seventeenth century: they recounted the conquest of the Normans over the Saxons, the Battle of Hastings in 1066, the invasion of England by troops under William the Conqueror, etc. Why did these discourses revive the memory of this past? They did so in order to underscore the fact that it was war that presided over the birth of the English State. The origin of the political domination exercised by English royalty and the nobility is impure. It was established through spilled blood, in the arbitrariness of a battle, in the enslavement of one group by another. Consequently, the English Crown is illegitimate; it is not legally entitled to govern. It does not represent the people, but rather a particular group of conquerors trying to maintain their domination over others.

According to Foucault, this type of discourse is important because it shows how the practice of historiography was (and still can be) strategically deployed as a weapon against sovereignty.[10] The political order does not place the interests of citizens above its own interests; it is not a domain of the common, but of conquest. It is "the continuation of war by other means";[11] the laws and rights of the state are an extension of an original conflict. Its objective is to maintain an initial balance of power in favor of the winners: "according to this hypothesis, the role of political power is perpetually

---

10. Foucault, *Society Must be Defended*, 134–35. Foucault's gesture here is nearly identical to Pierre Bourdieu's "genetic approach" to the state. See Pierre Bourdieu, "Lecture of 10 January, 1991." In *On the State: Lectures at the Collège de France, 1989-1992*, translated by David Fernbach (London: Polity Press, 2014).

11. Foucault, *Society Must be Defended*, 15.

to use a sort of silent war to reinscribe that relationship of force, and to reinscribe it in its institutions, economic inequalities, language, and even in the bodies of individuals."[12]

By disclosing war as a permanent feature of social and political relations, this genealogical approach almost necessarily calls for insurrection: by refusing to consider the sovereign as our representative, by dispensing with the opaque origins of the state and thereby designating it an adversary, it lends revolt both logical and historical necessity. According to Foucault, it was precisely to silence this historicism, to defuse the subversive potential it contains, that Hobbes wrote *Leviathan*. And, for Foucault, the entire Western philosophico-juridical tradition was more generally built upon the same fear of struggle and confrontation. It structures itself in opposition to those discourses that encode political relationships in terms of confrontation, which is to say discourses that reinscribe the state within this social war instead of acknowledging its superiority.

Concepts like the contract, right, transfer, and representation made it possible for Hobbes to create a different vision, another story, a different hermeneutical grid than that found in the works employing the historical discourse of conquest. For Hobbes, as soon as the defeated, the vanquished, the vulnerable chose life over death, once they yielded and ceased fighting, they effectively signed a contract in which the agreed to obey: "they [made] their victors their representatives and restored a sovereign to replace the one who was killed in the war."[13] In other words, it is not war and defeat that gave birth to the state in an extra-juridical and brutal fashion: it was the will of the vanquished to cease fighting. Sovereignty thus arises from "fear, the renunciation of fear, and the renunciation of the risk of death":

> It is this that introduces us into the order of sovereignty and into
> a juridical regime: of absolute power. The will to prefer life to
> death: that is what founds sovereignty, and it is as juridical and

---

12.   Ibid., 15–16.
13.   Ibid., 95.

legitimate as the sovereignty that was established through the
mode of institution and mutual agreement.[14]

Leviathan, as Foucault is well aware, shocked political thought
as a result of its radical posture, its praise of absolutism, and its
tendency to legitimize any established state authority. And although
many other political philosophers have developed theories that are
less authoritarian and accord less rights to the sovereign than did
Hobbes, political philosophers, argues Foucault, always prefer
granting too much power to the state, rather than not enough. In
other words, what is most interesting about studying the Hobbesian
apparatus is the extent to which it shows the discourse of political
theory as not only a reactive discourse, but necessarily the discourse
of the state: the contract, the general will, the citizen, politics, etc.,
are all concepts that function as a means of legitimation.

Consequently, there is nothing liberating in this paradigm. It
functions as a discourse of submission, a discourse of rulers, a discourse in the service of state rationality. It founds the juridical constitution of political sovereignty on the basis of an inaugural act of
subjugation, even self-subjugation, through which subjects are constituted as subjects wanting to be governed. This is exactly the opposite of a critical approach, which takes relations of subjugation as
its object and studies how these relations produce subjectivities.
Such relations should not, therefore, simply be presupposed or considered necessary: they must be situated at the center of critical
analysis. For it is through their deconstruction that they become
susceptible to providing emancipatory instruments for the governed.
In other words, it is necessarily outside of the framework of philosophy of right and the myth of the political that we must search for a
means of founding a theoretical practice of resistance, struggle, and
de-subjugation. It is only by exiting from political philosophy that
Foucault is able to search for a means of founding a practice of
resistance against neoliberalism, instead of opposing neoliberalism
with the concepts of political theory that condemn us to regress and

---

14.   Ibid., 95.

fall back upon those myths that produce the effects of subjectifica-
tion.

12

THE QUESTION OF
CIVIL DISOBEDIENCE

The Foucauldian deconstruction of political philosophy and the theory of right is not, of course, merely a historical discussion about the contributions of bourgeois and Enlightenment thought. It bears directly upon contemporary political concerns. In this regard, one of Foucault's targets is clearly traditional conservative philosophy, which has always employed the fictional autonomy of politics, the rational subject, and the rule of law against Marxism, against theories of struggle (and theories of class struggle in particular), and against sociological determinism.[1] But we should also recognize this controversy takes place within radical theory as well. It deals with questions concerning the instruments of critique, the possibility of producing a discourse for resisting the logic of the state, and how to support movements dedicated to de-subjugation and achieving greater freedom. For in Foucault's view, a practice that adopts and uses juridical categories to try to disqualify the state by appealing to the law, to citizenship, to a "universalism-to-come," etc., is condemned to remain within the regime of sovereignty: such a practice opposes one given state of power relations, but not power relations

---

1. See Didier Eribon, *D'une révolution conservatrice et de ses effets sur la gauche française* (Paris: Léo Scheer, 2007).

as such. In short, such a practice is built upon a system of subjugation it fails to call into question.

This was one of the central issues in the famous 1974 debate between Michel Foucault and Noam Chomsky on the question of civil disobedience.[2] During this polemic, Foucault still seems influenced by Marxist categories he would later question—though perhaps he is using these categories because the prefers to debate Chomsky on his own terms and within the system Chomsky adopts. In any case, one of the central questions of the debate is whether there exists something that could be described as the "foundations" of a worker's insurrection—or, indeed, for political opposition more generally: is it necessary to seek justification for anti-government mobilization? Can or should we think of such actions using juridical categories? Should we try to legitimize opposition by inscribing it within the horizon of legality, justice, and rationality?

The position adopted by Chomsky is the more classical, and the more reassuring. For him, it is necessarily in the name of the law, in the name of a purer justice, that the struggles of the oppressed must be carried out. Revolt against the state is undertaken on behalf of an ideal of a better society. In this sense, then, any discourse characterizing oppositional action as "illegal" must be refuted. This qualification is based on the ratification of a definition of justice, and of the law, as it is imposed by the established political order. According to Chomsky, however, it is the class struggle that has right on its side—true, rational right, and the law thus justifies struggle—even if it is only according to an ideal conception of justice or a superior, future legality. It is thus the contemporary state, conversely, that is the true criminal: "when I do something which the state regards as illegal, I regard it as legal: that is, I regard the state as criminal."[3] In this context, Chomsky compares the class struggle to acts of resistance and disobedience against imperialist war, and especially the war in Vietnam:

2. See Noam Chomsky, *The Chomsky-Foucault Debate*, edited by John Rajchman (New York: New Press, 2006).
3. Ibid., 48.

> In fact there are interesting elements of international law, for
> example, embedded in the Nuremberg principles and the United
> Nations Charter, which permit, in fact I believe, *require*, the
> citizen to act against his own state in ways which the state will
> falsely regard as criminal. Nevertheless, he's acting legally, be-
> cause international law also happens to prohibit the threat or use
> of force in international affairs, except under some very narrow
> circumstances, of which, for example, the war in Vietnam is not
> one. This means that in the particular case of the Vietnam War,
> which interests me the most, the American state is acting in a
> criminal capacity. And the people have the right to stop crimi-
> nals from committing murder. Just because the criminal happens
> to call your action illegal when you try to stop him, it doesn't
> mean it *is* illegal.[4]

Chomsky is thus inscribed with the juridico-deductive axiomatic in
a manner that resembles Rousseau and the French Revolution. It is
unthinkable, for Chomsky, not to attempt to ground and legitimize
revolts—if only to be able to distinguish between those revolts that
are "just" and those that are not. We must always have some criter-
ion of judgment, a standard for evaluating reality—and it is precisely juridical rationality and a conception of right that enables this: a
revolt is considered legitimate or just when it is possible to inscribe
it within the framework of a future legality—or, better, to submit it
to such a legality—and thereby define the present situation as illegal.[5]

Foucault does not, of course, completely reject the idea that this
framework can, from a certain point of view, provide instruments of
resistance. For Foucault, however, the fact remains that using such a
conceptual apparatus to justify social or political struggle, without
questioning the apparatus itself, is highly problematic, for the concepts of "law," "justice," and "subject of right" are inscribed within
the very system these struggles claim to fight. Thus, in the end, they
will necessarily reproduce the effects of subjugation. Far from pro-

---

4. Ibid., 48–49.
5. See Sandra Laugier and Albert Ogien, *Pourquoi désobéir en démocratie?* (Paris:
La Découverte, 2010).

viding us with the means to undo or deconstruct the mechanisms of political sovereignty, they ratify, prolong, and naturalize such apparatuses:

> It seems to me that the idea of justice in itself is an idea which in effect has been invented and put to work in different types of societies as an instrument of a certain political and economic power or as a weapon against that power. But it seems to me that, in any case, the notion of justice itself functions within a society of classes.[6]

And it is for this reason, as Foucault concludes further:

> Contrary to what you think, you can't prevent me from believing that these notions of human nature, of justice, of the realization of the essence of human beings, are all notions and concepts which have been formed within our civilization, within our type of knowledge and our form of philosophy, and that as a result form part of our class system; and one can't, however regrettable it may be, put forward these notions to describe or justify a fight which should—and shall in principle—overthrow the very fundaments of our society.[7]

---

6. *The Chomsky-Foucault Debate*, 54–55.
7. Ibid., 57–58.

13

BEYOND *LAISSEZ FAIRE*

How do we escape the discourse of the state? How do we resist the state without recourse to the weapons, vocabularies, and concepts that inscribe us within the state apparatus and constitute us, *eo ipso*, as obedient subjects, as subjects submitted beneath a sovereign? These are the questions Foucault sought to answer in the mid-1970s. These questions are of great importance, and not only in terms of developing a new, alternative theory of power that is opposed to its traditional conception. It is also a matter of reflecting on the means available to us to escape foundational theories, break with juridical rationality, and thereby free ourselves from the myths of the juridical and the political. Foucault seeks to adopt a new attitude here: to not stand, like most political philosophers, on the side of the state and those who govern, but rather on the side of the governed, their struggles, and their aspirations.

In many respects, it seems to me Foucault's interest in liberalism and neoliberalism can only be understood in this context. For if, according to Foucault, neoliberalism introduced a rupture in the history of thought, it is because it shattered the constitutive elements of political philosophy and juridical normativity. In other words, concepts such as "the market," "economic rationality," "*homo eco-nomicus*," etc., were perceived by Foucault as extremely powerful critical instruments for disqualifying the paradigm of right, the law, the contract, the General Will, etc. This paradigm opens up the possibility of speaking a language other than the language of the state.

In *The Birth of Biopolitics*, Foucault thus opposes two major traditions of analyzing power and sovereignty. On the one side, there is the axiomatic juridico-deductive tradition, the Rousseauian path of which I have spoken previously. But there is another absolutely alternative tradition, the origin of which dates back to English radicalism. This tradition invented a new way of interrogating the state by opposing, fundamentally, *la raison d'État*. Its rejection of sovereignty is its major characteristic. It does not subscribe to the categories of right. It does not pose the question of the legitimacy of state action. It is interested in something very different, something it calls "utility."

When we analyze governmental practice, the usual attitude consists in asking if this or that action is "legitimate," whether state action has a legal basis. Political economy, however, conceived a new mode of problematization: it examines governmental practice on the basis of its *effects*. Foucault considers the example of taxes. The liberals, or the English radicals, do not pose the problem by asking what authority the sovereign has to levy taxes. Rather, they simply ask:

> What will happen if, at a given moment, we raise a tax on a particular category of persons or a particular category of goods? What matters is not whether or not this is legitimate in terms of law, but, what its effects are and whether they are negative. It is then that the tax in question will be said to be illegitimate or, at any rate, to have no raison d'être. The economic question is always to be posed within the field of governmental practice, not in terms of what may found it by right, but in terms of its effects.[1]

According to Foucault, the essential feature of English radicalism and liberalism is its ability to have freed itself from the statist men-

---

1.   Foucault, *The Birth of Biopolitics*, 15.

tality—because of an acute mistrust of leaders and rulers. This tradition thus produced an original method of analyzing politics in a non-political manner. It does not think, in contrast to the revolutionaries and theorists of the Enlightenment, in terms of right, legitimacy, contract, etc. Rather, it evaluates the law from the point of view of its utility or its non-utility, which is to say its harmful or beneficial consequences.

Contemporary neoliberalism, Foucault insists, is inscribed in this lineage. Neoliberalism takes up this mode of questioning, this way of problematizing governmental practice, but it radicalizes it and generalizes it—as is particularly evident in the United States. Since the 1960s, the neoliberal critique of the state framed the market, or market rationality, as an instrument for evaluating government. The neoliberals erected a sort of "permanent economic tribunal"[2] for government, designed to judge and weigh all of its activities on behalf of the law of the market. In other words, the market form is permanently opposed to the government within the neoliberal *dispositif*. It is no longer the case, as it was with classical liberalism, of asking the state to adopt a *laissez-faire* attitude with respect to the market, but rather a case of "do not *laissez-faire* government" in the name of the market:

> The economic grid will or should make it possible to test governmental action, gauge its validity, and to object to activities of the public authorities on the grounds of their abuses, excesses, futility, and wasteful expenditure. In short, the economic grid . . . involves scrutinizing every action of the public authorities in terms of the game of supply and demand, in terms of efficiency with regard to the particular elements of this game, and in terms of the cost of intervention by the public authorities in the field of the market. In short, it involves criticism of the governmentality actually exercised which is not just a political or juridical criticism; it is a market criticism, the cynicism of a market criticism opposed to the action of the public authorities.[3]

---

2. Ibid., 247.
3. Ibid., 246.

Foucault obviously does not ignore the dangers this type of practice can pose; elsewhere he cites, as an example, the American Enterprise Institute—whose objective is to evaluate politics using a cost-benefit analysis—as a hot spot of Republican reaction against the welfare-state and social legislation passed by the Democrats.

However, what is fundamentally of interest for Foucault, in my view, is neoliberalism's gesture of insubordination—or even, one might say, the unlikely *coup d'État* the neoliberals accomplished. Discourses that remain imprisoned within the categories of traditional politics remain inscribed within the system of sovereignty. Such discourses might certainly invoke these rights in order to set limits on the exercise of government power (whenever certain governmental actions appear illegitimate or extra-judicial), but they can never question the basis of public authority, challenge the state-form itself, or contest its fundamental claim to make us obey. By refusing juridical categories, and thereby dissolving governmental practice within the economy, neoliberalism goes much further. It is not content to limit the power of the sovereign: "to a certain extent, [*homo economicus*] strips the sovereign of power."[4] The neoliberal problematic tries to disqualify the sovereign entirely. Economic calculation demystifies politics and brings it down off its pedestal. The idea that we should obey the law because it is legitimate, because it is the embodiment of a juridical and general "will," is rejected. Neoliberalism does not recognize sovereignty as a special authority, and it subjects the latter to utilitarian evaluation.

Sovereignty is not endowed with value in and of itself: it is of value only if its benefits outweigh its costs—and thus the very idea of obedience, of respect for authority, has no meaning within the neoliberal framework.

This is the reason why Foucault insists the economic and juridico-political worlds are "heterogeneous and incompatible."[5] *Homo juridicus*, the subject of right, is the subject who accepts negativity, transcendence, limitation, and obedience to the law. But *homo eco-*

---

4.   Ibid., 292.
5.   Ibid., 282.

nomicus never renounces his interests: he is inscribed within an egoistic mechanism, but one totally devoid of transcendence; he never stops maximizing his utility on behalf of demands that are said to be superior.[6] Accordingly, *homo economicus* renders the constitution of a political unity defined by the existence of a sovereign impossible—because this process demands the renunciation of one's rights, or the transfer of one's rights to someone else: "*homo economicus* is integrated into the system of which he is a part, into the economic domain, not by a transfer, subtraction, or dialectic of renunciation, but by a dialectic of spontaneous multiplication,"[7] which is that of the free and decentralized market, the space of exchange where the will of everyone is reconciled with the will of others. Neoliberalism thus substitutes contracts for moral or social constraints; it favors forms of association (in the plural) to the detriment of state organization.[8] And this is why neoliberalism can support certain utopian communities—such as that described by Robert Nozick, for example, who defines the neoliberal society as an indeterminate space in which everyone can be seditious and create new worlds.[9]

Homo economicus thus appears, in the truest sense, as an ungovernable being. I am well aware Foucault also described *homo economicus* as "eminently governable"[10] later in his lectures, but this is not the same type of governability at work in traditional political and legal theory—which Foucault makes explicit when he remarks how "*homo economicus* strips the sovereign of power."[11] Neoliberalism does not, of course, prevent human agents from engaging with other incentive structures, such as those involving price signals and other such market mechanisms. But its governmental

---

6. We can see, therefore, that it is not a question of advancing a crude criticism of the state on behalf of the individual: for both the juridical tradition and the economic tradition are individualistic traditions. But they do not produce the same concept of the individual: the individual is constructed as an obedient subject, in the one case, and as an agent affirming its interests in the other.

7. Foucault, *The Birth of Biopolitics*, 292.

8. See Henri Arvon, *Les Libertariens américains* (Paris: PUF, 1983).

9. Robert Nozick, *Anarchy, State, and Utopia* (New York: Basic Books, 1974).

10. Foucault, *The Birth of Biopolitics*, 270.

11. Ibid., 292.

powers act on the surface of *homo economicus*, on its external behavior through variations in incentive, and this is completely different from the paradigm of obedience. It is the same word, but it is not
the same process, and it is not something I think we can truly call
"government." *Homo economicus* should not therefore be viewed as
simply a model or tool used to obtain knowledge within the field of
economics. It is a polemical instrument: a weapon constructed, sys-
tematized, and theorized to unleash a critical discourse against the
state, and challenge the exercise of sovereignty. Neoliberalism, in
this sense, constitutes one of the forms in which, at a given moment,
the "assertion or claim of the independence of the governed vis-à-
vis governmentality" is enunciated.[12] And this is why neoliberalism
holds so much promise for Foucault. By opposing juridical logic to
economic logic, and *homo juridicus* to *homo economicus*, Foucault
succeeds in highlighting the extent to which power works to induce
obedience, resignation, and negativity in contemporary societies.
Escaping this governmental apparatus is an urgent task, one that
requires the invention of non-political methods of challenging politics. Foucault invites us to rethink the conditions under which emancipatory practice is developed—and implores us to consider the fact
that any critique of neoliberalism that exalts the law, the political, or
sovereignty is not only unsatisfactory but, on the contrary, potentially regressive and reactionary.

---

12.   Ibid., 42.

14

HOMO ECONOMICUS, PSYCHOLOGY, AND THE DISCIPLINARY SOCIETY

I would like to conclude this examination of Foucault's inquiry into neoliberalism by evoking one last aspect of his analysis. This aspect of his analysis is more difficult to address than those discussed previously because Foucault only dedicates a few pages to it in the course of his lectures. Accordingly, it may seem as if this dimension of his inquiry is merely a side issue and of only minor importance. Yet this issue seems central to me inasmuch as it refers to questions of the norm, the operation of disciplinary power, and the parallel issue of psychology, psychiatry, and psychoanalysis in contemporary societies.

This dimension of Foucault's analysis traverses two lectures in *The Birth of Biopolitics* dedicated to rational choice theory, *homo economicus* as an economic model, and the work of Gary Becker in particular. The objective of these lectures is to underscore the fact that neoliberalism cannot be viewed as merely a philosophical or political doctrine: we must equally consider the extent to which neoliberalism facilitated considerable epistemological renewal in the discipline of economics.

As Foucault observes, economic analysis, from Adam Smith to the mid-twentieth century, was defined by its *object*: it was the study of the mechanisms of the production, exchange, and distribution of wealth. Economics was a science concerned with a particular portion of reality, that is, "economic reality," characterized, for example, by consumption, investment, the division of labor, growth, etc. But neoliberalism, especially its American variant, proposed an alternative conception. It did not define economics according to an object, but according to an activity: economics as the science of rational choice. It is defined as "the study and analysis of the ways in which scarce means are allocated to competing ends."[1] As Foucault puts it more precisely:

> In other words, we have scarce means, and we do not have a single end or cumulative ends for which it is possible to use these means, but ends between which we must choose, and the starting point and general frame of reference for economic analysis should be the way in which individuals allocate these scarce means to alternative ends.[2]

This redefinition of economics—first formulated by Lionel Robbins[3]—played a considerable role in the history of thought. It inaugurated a movement referred to as the economic imperialism of the social sciences. At the moment when economics redefined itself as the science of rational choice, as the study of how individuals decide to allocate their resources toward one end rather than another, it gave itself the right to examine every facet of human behavior, not only those behaviors that have been traditionally coded as "economic": to have children or not, to marry or not to marry, to take care of one's health or not, to take drugs or not . . . these actions all constitute so many decisions based on an explicit or implicit calculus and, therefore, fall within the domain of economic analysis.

One of neoliberalism's great victories thus issued from its proposition to decipher an entire panoply of non-market realities and rela-

1. Foucault, *The Birth of Biopolitics*, 222.
2. Ibid.
3. "Economics is the science which studies human behaviour as a relationship between ends and scarce means which have alternative uses." Lionel Robbins, *An Essay on the Nature and Significance of Economic Science* (New York: New York University Press, 1984 [1932]), 16.

tionships using market terms. Human beings are no longer thought of as compartmentalized entities who use economic reasoning for economic actions and then obey all manner of social, moral, political, psychological, or ethical values in other domains of life. Human beings are now thought of as unified, coherent entities. They apply economic calculation to all aspects of life; they behave, so to speak, like individual entrepreneurs continually trying to maximize their utility under the constraints of the resources at their disposal. Neoliberalism, therefore, proposes to use the model of *homo economicus* as a grid of intelligibility for understanding every actor and every action.[4]

We know the conception of the human as a rational being is one of the most disparaged aspects of economics in its "orthodox" version. It is often invoked as a foil. It is proof that neoliberalism pedals a mutilated view of humans as predominately self-interested, materialistic, and egoistic beings. It passes us off as cold monsters and calculating machines (to borrow Marcel Mauss' expression) when we are, in fact, complex beings defined by affects, emotions, passions, spiritual values, etc. Even in those domains of critical theory that frame individualism as a leftist value and promote individualism as an emancipatory project, it is striking that the individual brandished against *homo economicus* tends to be an anti-materialistic and anti-utilitarian individual endowed with sense, affectivity, and morality—a form of subjectivity surprisingly resonate with Christian discourse.

In *The Birth of Biopolitics*, Foucault does not resort to these modes of disqualification. On the contrary, he ruminates on the productivity of *homo economicus*, and on the fecundity of this schema for analyzing human behavior. And in this context, Foucault elaborates this thought through a very precise example: the question of crime, punishment, and penal policy as studied by the Nobel

---

4. See Gary Becker, *The Economic Approach of Human Behavior* (Chicago: University of Chicago Press, 1976), 14.

Prize–winning American economist Gary Becker in his celebrated 1969 article, "Crime and Punishment."[5]

It was clearly not by chance that Foucault chose such an example. We know the study of "deviance," the ways the deviant is labeled, constructed, and problematized constituted, for Foucault, one of the privileged instruments through which the operation of disciplinary power in contemporary societies is revealed.

In his courses given at the Collège de France in the mid-1970s entitled *Psychiatric Power*[6] and *Abnormal*[7]—and, of course, in *Discipline and Punish*[8]—Foucault's work was devoted to analyzing the metamorphosis of the penal system and the representation of the criminal at the end of the nineteenth century. One of the themes that runs through this work is his attempt to show the point at which the introduction of psychiatric expertise within the judicial system radically transformed the perception and treatment of criminals. The criminal was no longer conceived as a simple "offender," by which Foucault means an individual who is defined by his actions, by what he has done. Rather, psychiatric expertise introduces the idea that crime is also—and perhaps even above all—the manifestation of perversion, deviant tendencies, immoral impulses, and disordered inclinations contracted during childhood. Accordingly, crime is no longer merely a transgression of the law. It is a profoundly psychological event. The criminal is no longer conceived as a normal subject but construed as a "distinctive personality type." As Foucault puts it in *Abnormal*:

> Expert psychiatric opinion allows the offense, as defined by the law, to be doubled with a whole series of other things that are not the offense itself but a series of forms of conduct, of ways of being that are, of course, presented in the discourse of the

5. Gary Becker, "Crime and Punishment: An Economic Approach." *Journal of Political Economy*, vol. 76, no. 2 (1969): 169–217.
6. Michel Foucault, *Psychiatric Power: Lectures at the Collège de France, 1973-1974*, translated by Graham Burchell (New York: Picador, 2008).
7. Michel Foucault, *Abnormal: Lectures at the Collège de France, 1974-1975*, translated by Graham Burchell (New York: Picador, 1999).
8. Michel Foucault, *Discipline and Punish*, translated by Alan Sheridan (New York: Vintage Books, 1977).

psychiatric expert as the cause, origin, motivation, and starting point of the offense. In fact, in the reality of judicial practice they constitute the substance, the very material to be punished.[9]

This psychiatric *dispositif* is historically significant because it fundamentally redefined the representation of the criminal and the meaning of crime in relation to the law. Crime is now something more than mere illegal conduct. It is the consequence and manifestation of an irregularity in relation to ethical norms:

> Expert psychiatric opinion makes it possible to constitute a psychologico-ethical double of the offense. That is to say, it makes it possible to delegalize the offense as formulated by the code, in order to reveal behind its double, which resembles it like a brother or a sister, I don't know, and which makes it not exactly an offense in the legal sense of the term, but an irregularity in relation to certain rules, which may be physiological, psychological, or moral. . . . In fact, psychiatry does not really set out an explanation of the crime but rather the thing itself to be punished that the juridical system must bite on and get a hold of.[10]

In other words, the emergence of psychiatry, of psychiatric power, thickened the typologies established by the law. The separation between licit and illicit was redoubled by a host of new meanings: it now also demarcates moral and immoral, normal and abnormal, etc. The juridical system is no longer dealing with an "offender," but rather a "delinquent." Crime is no longer apprehended from a strictly legal point of view, but from a psychologico-moral point of view as well. In this sense, psychiatric power creates a new type of subject—*homo criminalis*—who is characterized less by his actions and more by his personality.

What is implied here is not only the fact that it is now impossible to deal with a criminal without knowing his entire biography and way of life (we are no longer content to ask what the delinquent did,

---

9. Foucault, *Abnormal*, 15.
10. Ibid., 16.

we must interrogate who they are) but also—and this is equally important—the criminal actually pre-dates his crime (and, in extreme cases, exists apart from it entirely) because, ultimately, this act merely constitutes the manifestation of a preexisting psychological and moral disorder.[11]

Foucault emphasizes the point at which this psychologization of criminality transformed the nature of punishment and the role of the judiciary: their goal is no longer to merely suppress an action or redress an injury. They are now integrated into an apparatus tasked with caring for and rehabilitating the criminal. For one who is "abnormal" can no longer merely be punished in the penal sense of the term: they must be re-educated, corrected, and transformed. The reconceptualization of crime by psychiatry thus led to the introduction of a new type of power situated at the intersection of the medical and juridical establishments: the power of "normalization." And this new power did not, evidently, emerge from nowhere: it represents but one of those modalities through which disciplinary power, a modern technique of controlling and training individuals, was born.

One of the central ideas developed by Foucault from the mid-1970s onwards, as shown by Didier Eribon, is that the mechanics of power in our societies are consubstantially linked to the emergence and diffusion of the "psy-function," which is to say psychiatry, psychoanalysis, and concomitant notions of interiority, personality, familial unconscious, etc. Consequently, any radical critique of subjugating norms cannot avoid radical criticism of the psychological conception of the subject.[12] And this is precisely why Foucault was so intrigued by neoliberalism, especially when it came to its analysis of crime. It is a methodology that is defined by a fundamental anti-psychologism, and in fact it seemed to suggest the possibility of deconstructing psychiatric discourse and the disciplinary paradigm itself.

11. Michel Foucault, *Discipline and Punish* (New York: Vintage Books, 1977), 286.
12. See Didier Eribon, *Échapper à la psychanalyse* (Paris: Léo Scheer, 2005).

In fact, anti-psychologism is the fundamental methodological premise of neoclassical economics. It forms its negative foundation. Gary Becker asserts this in an extremely forceful manner in the introduction to *The Economic Approach to Human Behavior* (1976). Modern economics, he insists, attempts to break with all those sciences claiming to account for individual behavior by invoking tastes, moral inclinations, psychology, culture, identity, etc. For Becker, this is a simplistic attitude. It leads to lazy and often quasi-tautological explanations. But above all, analyses of this kind rely on unobservable realities and "internal" mental characteristics that are more presupposed than objectively established. This is why economics, for Becker, must begin from the inverse postulate. It presupposes identity between all individuals: all individuals have comparable tastes and aversions.[13] Consequently, explaining differences in behavior by referencing variant "psychological" traits is prohibited as a matter of principle. One may account for the variability of practices only by evoking the environmental differences individuals confront, or the dissimilarity of the contexts in which they live. In other words, economics treats actors as superimposable *homo economici* situated within distinctive environments. This methodology enables the politicization of almost every dimension of human life.

It is thus easy to understand how the application of *homo economicus* to crime radically transformed the perception of this phenomenon and its "causes": under no circumstances does anyone presuppose the criminal differs from those who "conform." The criminal will not be assigned psychological characteristics or singular, perverse inclinations. Criminal activity and, conversely, legal behavior is not the manifestation of anything inscribed within the psyche. The choice simply depends on the objective incentives individuals encounter: the benefits (or the costs) they are likely to accrue by performing one act rather than another. Crime is thus a rational act. A criminal is merely someone who accepts the risk of punishment because, given the concrete situation in which they are

---

13.   See George J. Stigler and Gary S. Becker, "De Gustibus Non Est Disputandum." *American Economic Review*, vol. 67, no. 2 (March 1977): 76–90.

placed, anticipation of the proceeds of crime is greater than the anticipated loss they will suffer if they are arrested and punished.[14]

The significance of this type of analysis is, first of all, to scale back conceptions of crime and rid crime of the influence of moral and moralizing categories. But above all, neoclassical economics, and Gary Becker in particular, wrenches the criminal from the clutches of the psychiatrist. Indeed, as Foucault puts it, if we define crime as:

> the action an individual commits by taking the risk of being punished by the law, then you can see that there is no difference between an infraction of the highway code and a premeditated murder. This also means that in this perspective the criminal is not distinguished in any way by or interrogated on the basis of moral or anthropological traits. The criminal is nothing other than absolutely anyone whatsoever.[15]

Neoliberal economics thus produces what Foucault calls the "anthropological erasure of the criminal."[16] It rejects the relevance of classifying individuals as either normal or abnormal, and it also rejects the distinctions between "born criminals, occasional criminals, the perverse and the not perverse, and recidivists," etc.[17] "All [these] distinctions," states Foucault, "are not important."[18] Consequently, neoliberalism destabilizes and potentially collapses the entire penal system insofar as the latter relies on the pathologization of the criminal and psychiatric power:

> You can see that in view of this the penal system will no longer have to concern itself with that split reality of the crime and the criminal. It has to concern itself with a conduct or a series of conducts which produce actions from which the actors expect a profit and which carry a special risk, which is not just the risk of

---

14. See Gary Becker, *The Economic Approach of Human Behavior*, 40–46. Also see from the same author, "The Economic Way of Looking at Life," Nobel Lecture, 1992.

15. Foucault, *The Birth of Biopolitics*, 253.

16. Ibid., 258.

17. Ibid., 259.

18. Ibid.

economic loss, but the penal risk, or that economic loss which is inflicted by the penal system. The penal system itself will not have to deal with criminals, but with those people who produce that type of action.[19]

It is therefore understandable why Foucault perceived neoliberalism as a radical critique of the very foundations of disciplinary power. For there is a consubstantial relationship between the disciplines and psychology: discipline is precisely that type of power that invests and establishes "psychisms." It corrects individuals from within through internal mechanisms of subjugation. This conceptualization appears, for example, in the redefinition of law in the work of Marcela Iacub, for whom law is increasingly becoming a symbolic apparatus designed to act on subjectivities and regulate consciousness rather than behavior.[20] The anti-psychologism of the economic model, however, disqualifies this paradigm of power. It does not act on the players: it may only intervene on the regulations of the field, on the variables of the environment. It extricates itself from the psyche and only considers the external coordinates individuals confront and to which they respond. In other words, neoliberal policy is not disciplinary. It embodies the attempt to resist this conception of power in the name of a different type of politics, a politics defined as purely and strictly "environmental." By redefining the terrain upon which power is able to legitimately intervene, neoliberalism, promotes a worldview, a conception of society, that has nothing to do with the project of the disciplinary society.

As Foucault insists at some length, the psychiatric codification of individuals as "abnormal" is consubstantially linked to the establishment of rehabilitating and normalizing mechanisms. In other words, the disciplinary society is built on the horizon of the norm. It valorizes conformity. It intervenes on individuals through procedures of internal subjugation designed to train, regulate, and condi-

---

19. Ibid., 253.
20. Marcela Iacub, "Le couple homosexuel, le droit et l'ordre symbolique." In *Le crime etait presque sexuel* (Paris: Flammarion, 2009). Also see "L'esprit des peines: la prétendue fonction symbolique de la loi et les transformations réelles du droit pénal en matière sexuelle." *L'Unebevué*, no. 20 (2002): 9–28.

tion them to play by the rules. The ideal disciplinary society is a society without crime, without deviance, without differences. Of course, one of the characteristics of disciplinary power is that it functions through individuation: it creates individuals. But this particularizing action is precisely designed to make disciplinary operations more effective.[21] Applying economic rationality to penal policy breaks with this way of viewing things. The neoliberal economists begin from a simple observation: reducing delinquency (which they call "enforcement") is of course beneficial. But, at the same time, it comes with a price—in terms of police personnel, the administration of justice, etc. Consequently, the very idea of eliminating crime, of identifying and punishing every criminal, is absurd. The cost of such a policy would be exorbitant and disproportionate: its costs would far exceed the benefits society would derive from this policy. The neoliberals thus reformulated the problem of penal policy. For them, it was no longer a question of asking, as was conventionally the case, how to fight and suppress crime. It is rather a question of determining, as Foucault cites Becker, "how many offenses should be permitted . . . [and] how many offenders should go unpunished?"[22]

What, then, is the ideal or the ultimate horizon of a neoliberal society? It is not, at all, a society of normalization. Rather, the ideal for these economists, according to Foucault, is "society does not have a limitless need for compliance. Society does not need to conform to an exhaustive disciplinary system. A society finds that it has a certain level of illegality and it would find it very difficult to have this rate reduced indefinitely."[23] The neoliberal society does not, therefore, attempt to normalize and control individuals. It is a pluralistic society. It is characterized by a kind of "tolerance" accorded to individual "offenders" and minority practices. It doesn't try to eliminate "systems of difference" but rather tries to optimize them—

---

21. Foucault, *Discipline and Punish*, 198.
22. Foucault, *The Birth of Biopolitics*, 256.
23. Ibid.

through the establishment of decentralized systems of compensation between agents.

As Foucault is well aware, this social project is a pure intellectual construction. But his interaction with neoliberalism allows us to see what he meant when he proposed to use neoliberalism as a test, as a critical instrument for both thought and reality. For what Foucault emphasizes through the figure of *homo economicus* is a representation of the criminal act that departs from the representation envisioned and furnished by psychology or psychiatry. Consequently, psychology's claim to provide a faithful description of an empirical datum (the "concrete" subject, the subject as it really, truthfully is) collapses. For if constructions other than that provided by psychological discourse are conceivable, it means, at the very least, that psychology's version is but a construction. Comparatively, *homo economicus'* fictitious character renders visible the multitude of implicit hypotheses and arbitrary choices upon which psychiatric power is based—and thus the figure of the "abnormal" is likewise revealed as artificial.

Economic rationality, reasoning by model and by abstraction, is often criticized for its idealism. But we can see how this method constitutes a powerful instrument for denaturalization: it challenges our acceptance of reality. It forces us to break with our spontaneous adherence to our reality. Unlike the ethnographic approach, which dominates the social sciences and leads to pleonastic analyses of the world, economic rationality presents us with a means of imagining other ways of viewing and constructing reality. Neoclassical analysis offers us a means of undermining psychologizing and moralizing modes of thought, and of checking the relentless mechanics of disciplinary power. In other words, reconstituting neoliberalism's object is not an end in and of itself. It is a strategy. For Foucault, it is a theoretical tactic that offers insights into the form that an offensive against the disciplinary society might take. It is one possible locus of support for developing practices of de-subjugation.

BIBLIOGRAPHY

Althusser, Louis. *Politique et histoire.* Paris: Seuil, 2006.

Arendt, Hannah. *Lectures on Kant's Political Philosophy.* Chicago: University of Chicago Press, 1992.

———. *Qu'est-ce que la politique?* Paris: Seuil, 1995.

Audard, Catherine. *Qu'est-ce que le libéralisme?* Paris: Gallimard, 2009.

Becker, Gary. "Crime and Punishment: An Economic Approach." *Journal of Political Economy*, vol. 76, no. 2 (1969): 169–217.

———. *The Economic Approach of Human Behavior.* Chicago: University of Chicago Press, 1976.

———. "Nobel Lecture: The Economic Way of Looking at Behavior." *Journal of Political Economy*, vol. 101, no. 3 (1993): 385–409.

Berlin, Isaiah. *Conversations with Isaiah Berlin*, edited by Ramin Jahanbegloo. London: Peter Halban Press, 1992.

———. *The Sense of Reality.* New York: Farrar, Straus and Giroux, 1996.

———. *Four Essays on Liberty.* Oxford: Oxford University Press, 2002.

———. *Freedom and its Betrayal.* Princeton, NJ: Princeton University Press, 2014.

Bourdieu, Pierre. *Political Interventions: Social Science and Political Action*, translated by David Fernbach. London: Verso, 2008.

———. *On the State: Lectures at the Collège de France, 1989-1992*, translated by David Fernbach. London: Polity Press, 2014.

Brown, Wendy. "American Nightmare: Neoliberalism, Neoconservatism, and DeDemocratization." *Political Theory*, vol. 34, no. 6 (December 2006): 690–714.

Caré, Sébastien. *La Pensée libertarienne.* Paris: PUF, 2009.

Cassirer, Ernst. *The Question of Jean-Jacques Rousseau.* New Haven: Yale University Press, 1989.

Chomsky, Noam, and Michel Foucault. *The Chomsky-Foucault Debate: On Human Nature.* New York: New Press, 2006.

Derrida, Jacques. *Du droit à la philosophie.* Paris: Galilée, 1990.

Durkheim, Émile. *Le Contrat social de Rousseau.* Paris: Kimé, 2008.

———. *Hobbes à l'agrégation.* Paris: Éditions de l'EHESS, 2011.

Eribon, Didier. *Échapper à la psychanalyse.* Paris: Léo Scheer, 2005.

———. *D'une révolution conservatrice et de ses effets sur la gauche française.* Paris: Léo Scheer, 2007.

————. "Les frontières et le temps de la politique," concluding panel at the Sexual Nationalisms conference, Amsterdam, January 26–28, 2011, http://didiereribon. blogspot.com.

————. "Réponses et principes." *French Cultural Studies*, vol. 23, no. 2 (May 2012): 151–64.

Fabiani, Jean-Louis. *Les Philosophes de la République*. Paris: Minuit, 1988.

Foucault, Michel. *Discipline and Punish*, translated by Alan Sheridan. New York: Vintage Books, 1977.

————. "The Political Function of the Intellectual." *Radical Philosophy*, vol. 17 (Summer 1977).

————. *The History of Sexuality, Volume 1: An Introduction*, translated by Robert Hurley. New York: Vintage Books, 1979.

————. *Abnormal: Lectures at the Collège de France, 1974-1975*, translated by Graham Burchell. New York: Picador, 1999.

————. *Society Must be Defended: Lectures at the Collège de France, 1975-1976*, translated by David Macey. New York: Picador, 2003.

————. "The Meshes of Power." In *Space, Knowledge and Power: Foucault and Geography*. Hampshire: Ashgate Publishing, 2007.

————. *The Politics of Truth*, edited by Sylvère Lotringer. Los Angeles: Semiotext(e), 2007.

————. *Psychiatric Power: Lectures at the Collège de France, 1973-1974*, translated by Graham Burchell. New York: Picador, 2008.

————. *The Birth of Biopolitics: Lectures at the Collège de France, 1978-79*, translated by Graham Burchell. New York: Palgrave Macmillan, 2008.

Friedman, Milton. *Capitalism and Freedom*. Chicago: University of Chicago Press, 2002.

Guesnerie, Roger. *L'Économie de marché*. Paris: Le Pommier, 2006.

Habermas, Jürgen. *Between Facts and Norms: Contributions to a Discourse Theory of Law and Democracy*. Cambridge: MIT Press, 1998.

Harvey, David. *A Brief History of Neoliberalism*. Oxford: Oxford University Press, 2005.

Hayek, F. A. *The Road to Serfdom*. Chicago: University of Chicago Press, 2007 [1944].

————. "The Intellectuals and Socialism." *University of Chicago Law Review*, vol. 16, no. 3 (Spring 1949): 417–33.

————. *The Constitution of Liberty*. London: Routledge, 1960.

————. *Studies in Philosophy, Politics and Economics*. London: Routledge, 1967.

Iacub, Marcela. "L'esprit des peines: la prétendue fonction symbolique de la loi et les transformations réelles du droit pénal en matière sexuelle." *L'Unebévue*, no. 20 (2002): 928.

————. "Le couple homosexuel, le droit et l'ordre symbolique." In *Le crime était presque sexuel*. Paris: Flammarion, 2009.

————. *De la pornographie en Amérique*. Paris: Fayard, 2010.

Jones, Gareth Steadman. *Masters of the Universe: Hayek, Freidman, and the Birth of Neoliberal Politics*. Princeton: Princeton University Press, 2012.

Kant, Immanuel. *Kant: Political Writings*, edited by Hans Reiss. Cambridge: Cambridge University Press, 1991.

Kymlicka, Will. *Multicultural Citizenship: A Liberal Theory of Minority Rights*. Oxford: Clarendon Press, 1996.

Laugier, Sandra, and Albert Ogien. *Pourquoi désobéir en démocratie?* Paris: La Découverte, 2010.

Lemm, Vanessa, and Miguel Vatter. *The Government of Life: Foucault, Biopolitics and Neoliberalism*. New York: Fordham University Press, 2014.

Marx, Karl. "Critique of the Gotha Program." In *Marx-Engels Reader*, edited by Robert C. Tucker. New York: W.W. Norton, 1978.

Mill, John Stuart. *On Liberty and Other Essays*. Oxford: Oxford University Press, 1991.

Mirowski, Philip, and Dieter Plehwe (editors). *The Road From Mont Pèlerin: The Making of the Neoliberal Thought Collective*. Cambridge: Harvard University Press, 2009.

Nozick, Robert. *Anarchy, State, and Utopia*. New York: Basic Books, 1974.

Rawls, John. *A Theory of Justice*. Cambridge: Harvard University Press, 1999.

———. *Political Liberalism*. New York: Columbia University Press, 2005.

Robbins, Lionel. *An Essay on the Nature and Significance of Economic Science*. New York: New York University Press, 1984.

Rothbard, Murray. *The Ethics of Liberty*. Atlantic Highlands, NJ: Humanities Press, 1982.

Rousseau, Jean-Jacques. *The Social Contract*, translated by Christopher Betts. Oxford: Oxford University Press, 1994.

Skinner, Quentin. *Liberty Before Liberalism*. Cambridge: Cambridge University Press, 1998.

Stigler, George J., and Gary S. Becker. "De Gustibus Non Est Disputandum." *The American Economic Review*, vol. 67, no. 2 (March 1977): 76–90.

Veyne, Paul. *Foucault, sa pensée, sa personne*. Paris: Albin Michel, 2008.

Made in the USA
Las Vegas, NV
30 May 2024

90529319R00080